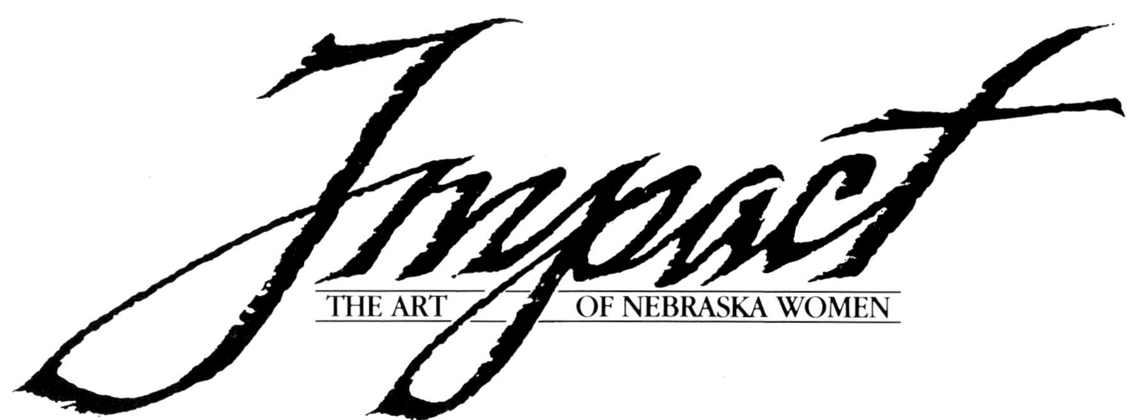

Impact

THE ART OF NEBRASKA WOMEN

Editor
Dora Hagge

Directors
Judy Greff
Sue Olson-Mandler
Amy Sadle

Contribution by Dr. Mary Lierley

Published by Impact, Inc.
with the support of the Nebraska Arts Council.

Designed by Joe Maguire

Design Supervisor: Kent Smith

Impact, Inc. is indebted to Kearney State College for its effort and support in the design of this book.

George W. Neubert, Director Sheldon Memorial Art Gallery, assisted in selection of artists and art works.

Photography copyright Larry S. Ferguson 1987
1701 Vinton St., Omaha, NE

Printed by Jacob North Printing Co., Inc., Lincoln, NE

The Nebraska Arts Council, a state agency, has supported this arts publication through its matching grants program funding by the Nebraska Legislature and the National Endowment for the Arts, a federal agency. The Nebraska Arts Council has a variety of grants and service programs to help support arts events throughout Nebraska. For information how the Nebraska Arts Council can be helpful to your community or organization, contact the Nebraska Arts Council, 1313 Farnam on-the-Mall, Omaha, NE 68102-1873. Phone: 402/554-2122.

ISBN 0-9619539-0-X (First Edition)
ISBN 0-9619539-1-8 (Collector's Edition)
Library of Congress Catalog Card Number 87-082216

Manufactured in the United States of America

EDITORS' STATEMENT

Years ago author Robert Louis Stevenson crossed Nebraska on a train. As he traveled for days across the flat expanses of golden wheat fields, he wrote that he felt as though he was at sea. As editors we feel much the same. The visual arts here seem imprinted by the uniqueness of the artist, and there is an aura of its origination. Nebraska inspires an earthiness, a freedom, and a diversity which is visible in this book. "IMPACT" is an opportunity to share the art of thirty-five exceptional women artists who were gleaned to represent a sea of golden creativity. We are grateful for the guidance we have received.

The Editors

Judy, Dora, Sue, Amy

Retrospective

Art is a reflection of time and place. This statement is pertinent to twentieth century Nebraska art as exemplified in the ensuing showcase that provides an opportunity to view a panoply of contemporary works created by Nebraska women —women recognized for significant contributions they are making in the visual arts. The exhibit is an ensemble of work shared through dedicated cooperative effort which depicts Nebraska history, makes social statements, renders nostalgic reminiscences, describes midwestern life both past and present, and those which are simply "art for art's sake." The viewer should not expect to see an isolated style of art, because as quoted from Norman Geske in ART AND ARTISTS IN NEBRASKA, "We cannot assume, local patriotism aside, that what has happened within the boundaries of this state is substantially different in kind or quality from similar artistic developments to the north, south, east, or west of us."

This introductory dialogue recounts past history of Nebraska women artists. In retrospect the writer has chosen a discriminatory selection of Nebraska women who were forerunners in the field of art. The initial women artists of the state, as was the case in many North American locations and pertained to male as well as female, were American Indians. As one might expect, most of their artistic products were primarily for utilitarian, status, and ritualistic purposes. Regardless of function, they have fine distinctive aesthetic qualities which we cherish today. Indian art that we savor in Joslyn Museum in Omaha or Stuhr Museum in Grand Island attest to this fact. Surely this art is a cultural implication of their tribal "time and place."

One of the first women about whom there is documentation is an Omaha Indian, In-stha-the-am-ba, Indian name for "Bright Eyes." Her legitimate English name was Susette LaFlesche Tibbles. She was born in 1854 at Bellevue and died in Lincoln in 1903. Following early training in a mission school, she was college educated in New Jersey. She is probably best remembered as interpreter for the Ponca Indians and as a public speaker, but she was also an artist, particularly an illustrator of books. Following an 1898 publication, the statement was made that her "illustrations are believed to be the first artistic work by an American Indian ever published."

Embroideries, sundry needlework, costume design when it was necessary for women to fashion and sew their own clothes, and china painting were popular artistic achievements for Nebraska pioneers, some of whom became professionally skilled. Most of these efforts were segments of women's roles properly exploited in the domestic and private sphere. A more unique type of art was pyrography which was especially popular about the turn of the century. It employed a method of woodburning to create an image on wooden boxes or plaques. Favorite subject matter of the time was Gibson girls, floweres, or Art Nouveau themes, some of which were extremely elaborate.

Many women artists were very versatile as noted by accounts of the works of Anna Field Cameron (1849-1931) originally from Illinois but who came to Chester, Nebraska, in Thayer County. She painted in both oil and watercolor, was a woodcarver, designer, and teacher. Accounts tell of her work being exhibited in Chicago at the World's Columbian Exposition, an international fair of 1893 where she received an award of excellence. The Nebraska State Historical Society has an oil painting signed by Gusta R. Strohm in 1888 with an accompanying statement that it is a painting of the Daniel Freeman homestead near Beatrice which was the first homestead in the United States. This is a very large painting and was probably painted from a photographic study. Another painting on display at the State Museum is a provincial farm scene painted by Sallie Cover in the 1880's. Her use of simplified shapes, the void of perspective, and highly saturated color all lend a Grandma

Grandma Moses atmosphere to this view of the Ellsworth Ball homestead in Garfield County.

In retrospect, one must not neglect some art educators who are also remembered as artists in their own right. First mention of art being taught at the University of Nebraska appeared in 1877 when art classes in painting and drawing were listed under the Agriculture Course which was part of the Industrial College. Sarah Wool Moore was listed in 1884-85 as teacher of painting, drawing, and lecturer on art history, and it was under her leadership a few years later that studies of "plastic anatomy and perspective" were added to the curriculum. She was one of the founders of the Hayden Art Club in 1881 which became the Nebraska Art Association in 1900. Cora Parker and Sarah Hayden (dates of both unknown) were also teachers at the University of Nebraska. These two women, as well as Alice Cleaver (1878-1944), studied under William Merritt Chase and became important portrait painters. A foremost painter born and educated in Lincoln and who studied at the Pennsylvania Academy of Fine Arts and Chicago Art Institute was Marion Canfield Smith (1873-1970). She taught at Kearney State College from 1905 until her retirement in 1943. She is particularly noted for portraits of Indians, both in oil and watercolors, made during her visits to the Rosebud Reservation in South Dakota. Kady Faulkner was another educator who taught at Nebraska University from 1930 to 1950. Her prints and paintings have received national attention as well as murals she executed in locations such as Union College, Lincoln, and the United States Post Office in Valentine, Nebraska.

Elizabeth Dolan (1887-1948) was Iowa-born but her family moved to Tecumseh and later to Lincoln where she studied at the University of Nebraska under Sarah Hayden. She also studied and traveled in Chicago, New York, and Europe, but never really became serious about her art until she was in her forty's. She is best known for her murals, many of which remain in prestigious locations including France and New York City. She painted fresco backgrounds in Morrill Hall on the University campus, most of them very large. She also did murals as private commissions in several Lincoln homes and one in the State Capitol building titled "Spirit of the Prairie" completed in 1930 and selected shortly afterward as one of the best mother-and-child paintings in America. This painting is quoted as capturing the "mood of courage displayed by Nebraska's settlers." It may be viewed on the north wall of the Law Library. She painted this mural for an absurdly small fee because, even though she had received commissions on the East coast and in Europe, she remained a loyal and dedicated Nebraskan. So in reality, she donated the product of her talents to her peers and future generations.

Even though Jeanne Reynal was not a Nebraskan nor did she consider herself one, it behooves one to mention her in the Nebraska art scene. She was born in 1903 in White Plains, New York, and died during the present decade. She came from New York state in 1967 to create two large mosaics for the Great Hall in the State Capitol. These are permanent acquisitions about which there was a great deal of controversy because of their extremely abstract qualities. Along with others they were installed in observance of Nebraska's one-hundredth birthday, as statehood had been granted in 1867. One of the Reynal mosaics is titled the "Blizzard of 1888" and is a chilling portrayal of a schoolroom's courageous struggle for survival amid the raging snowstorm . . . (the) chips and pieces brood or sparkle in their shadows, bleach themselves in reflected light." The other is titled "Tree Planting" which is described as a "bold, brilliant image of the magnificent blossoming of trees on the Nebraska plain."

Thus, it is with this smattering of information that we have a glimpse of an earlier Nebraska. The following unique exhibition provides a rewarding reflection from women artists of the present day - their personal extension of time and place.

Dr. Mary Lierley

My work is a window for me.

Through it I can perceive my strengths and weaknesses, my fears and hopes.

Making work feels good.

It can be physically and mentally challenging.

It can be spiritually rewarding.

I want my work to reflect this.

I want to make objects which have a sense of presence rather than of place.

I want images that mirror who I am.

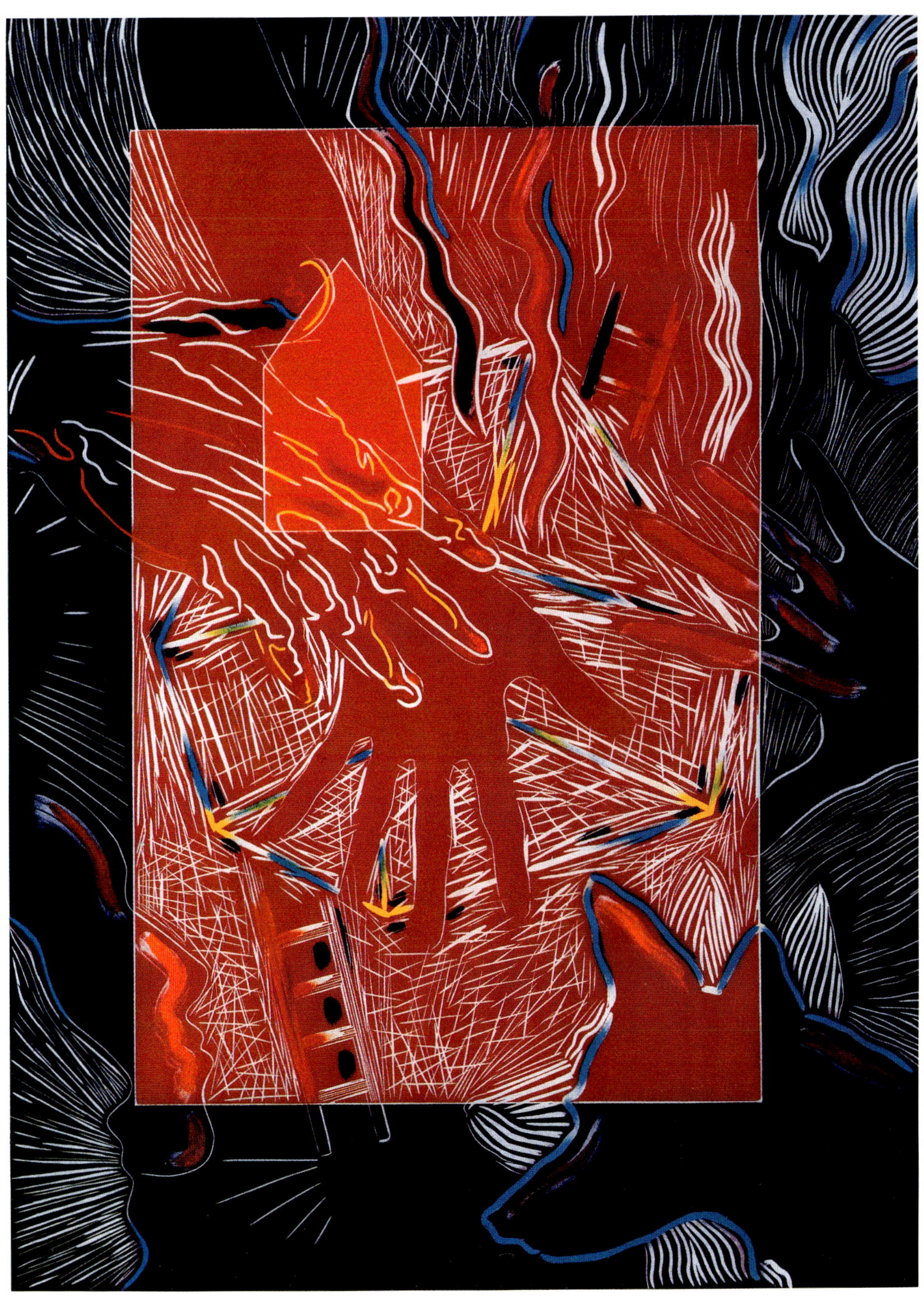

Watching Mary Day, 33 x 25 in., monoprint.

When I started using pastels I found what I had been seeking in all of my years as an artist. Pastels afforded me a way to paint the beautiful colors that gave me so much joy. With color I could express the beauty I was seeing. The longer I worked with them, the more I found I could do with them. I could put one color on top of another. I could put the colors side by side. I could cross-hatch with them. Always they would respond, and remain clear and beautiful, and say what I wanted to say.

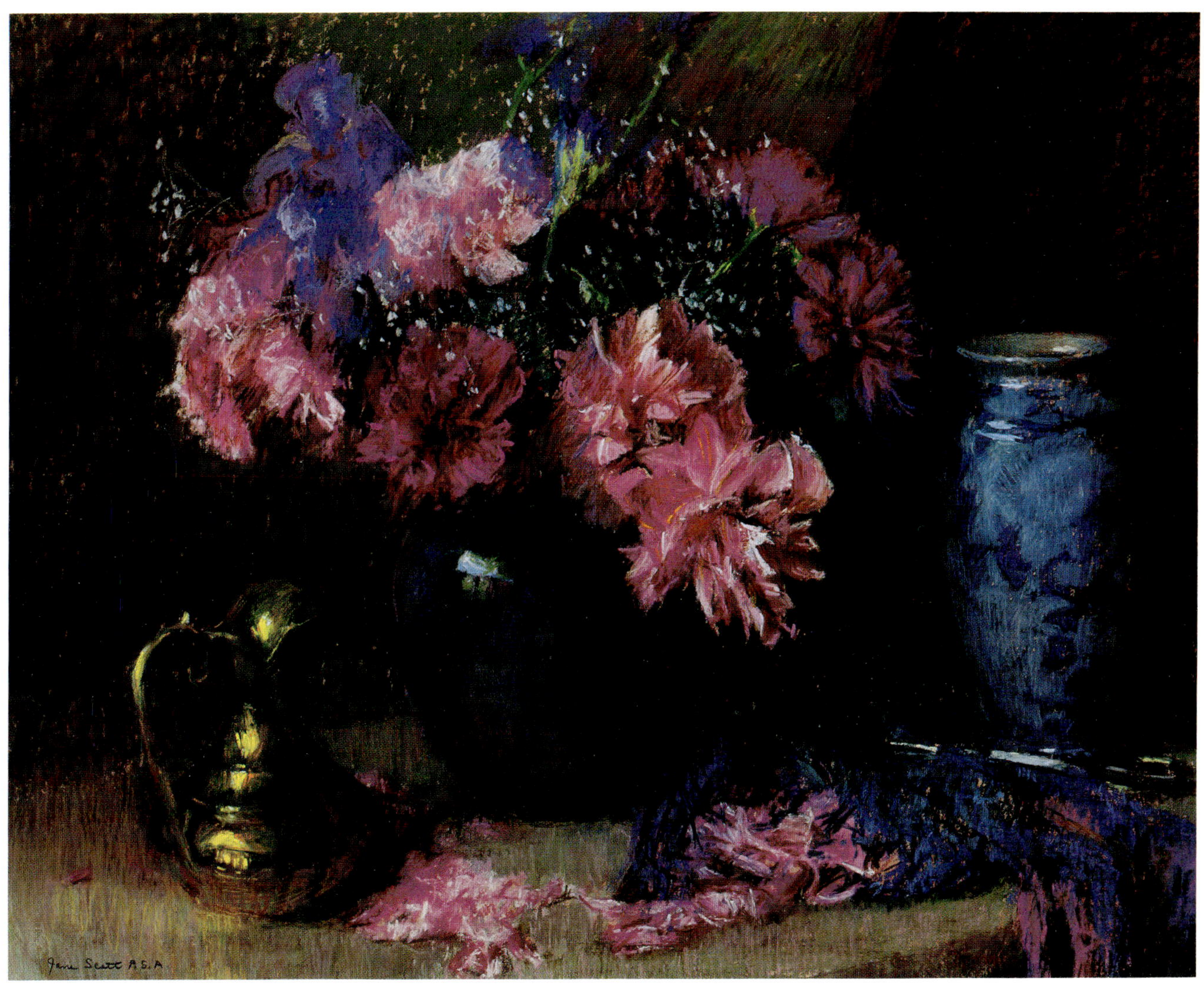

Peonies Jane Scott, 22 x 28 in., pastel.

I dream in color.

My surrounding world motivates my desire to create.

My mind gathers and conceives.

Once the concept is formed, it is all consuming.

The sum of my labors, selects and designs.

Striving for personal satisfaction is my goal.

Part of my soul is left on the painted surface.

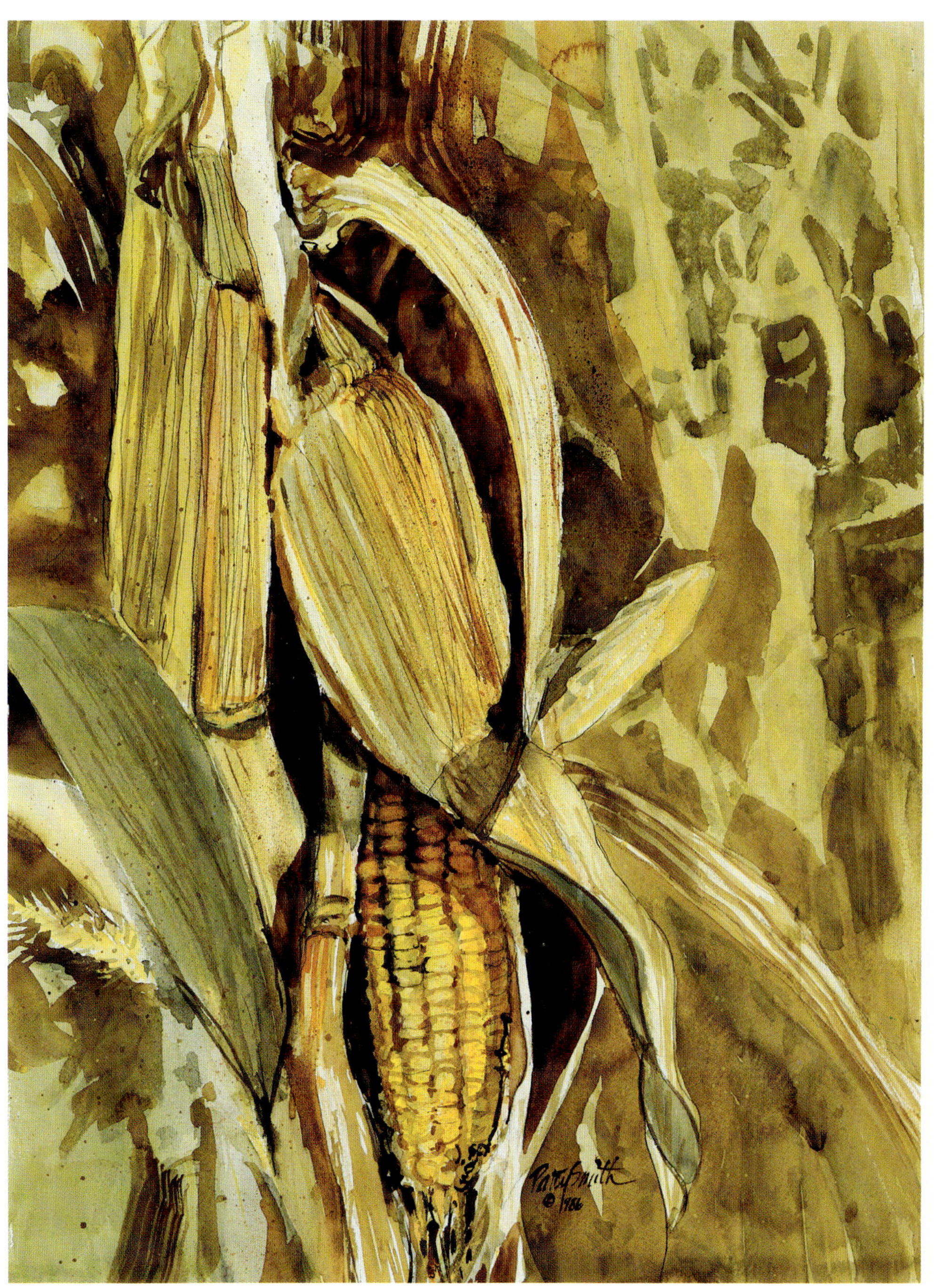

Ears and Stalks Patsy Smith, 28 x 20 in., watercolor.

My reputation as an artist has been greatly influenced by my bold use of color and unique layering technique in a typically subtle medium.

My work has been described as a combination of abstract expressionism and realistic landscapes. I paint from landforms, although my work has an ambiguous quality. Is it abstract or realistic? Is it a river or a road? Is it an evening sky or a morning sky? Is it a landscape or is it color?

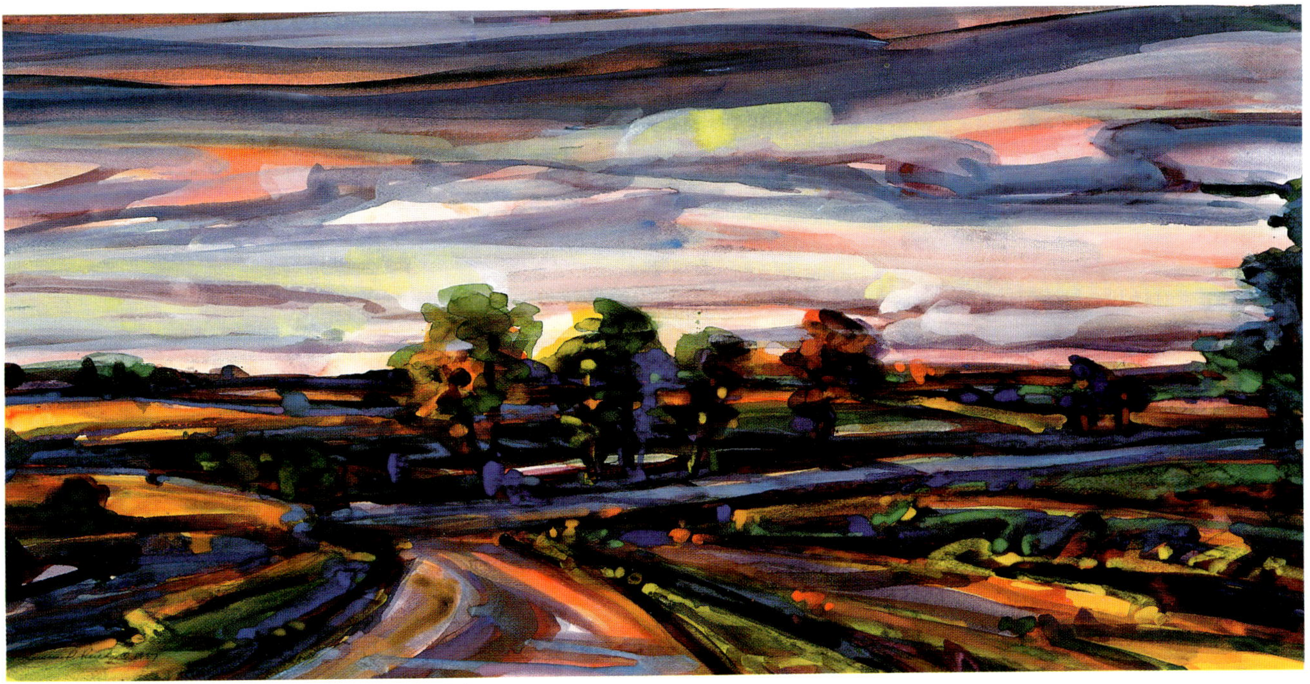

Prairie Steppes, II   Susan P. Puelz, 24 x 44 in., watercolor.

If I'm not good at verbally expressing myself,
perhaps my art work will speak for me.
There is so much feeling involved,
how can I tell someone else?

Yesterday, when the sun came out after the storm,
the color of the sky was so beautiful-it spoke of joy and hope.
It warmed my heart.
How can I say this in my painting?
I must try.

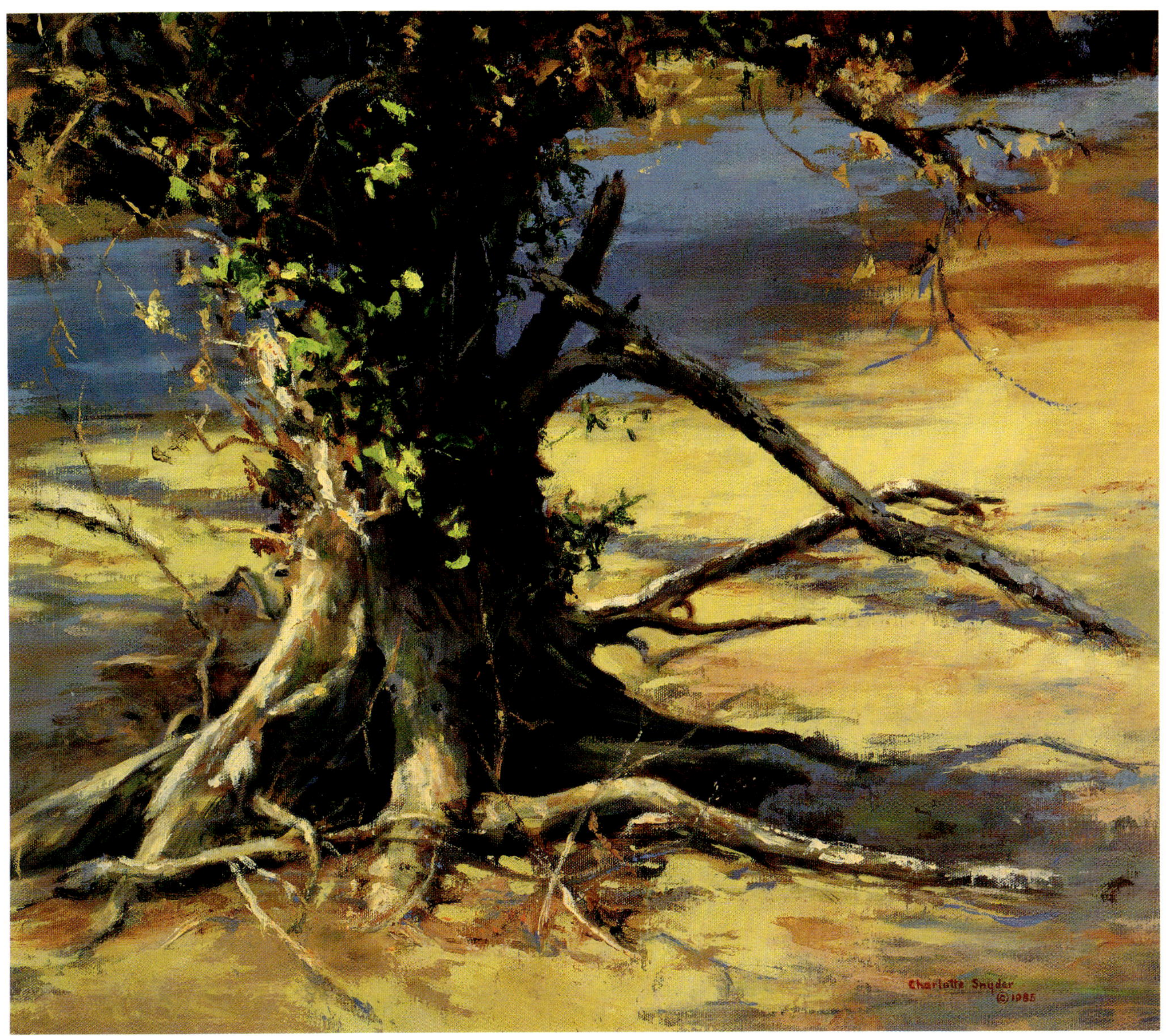

Tree Charlotte S. Snyder, 19 x 23 in., alkyd.

Some of my paintings are personal, intuitive, and symbolic statements of my feelings. Others are observations of my environment.

Farmers standing with thumbs hooked through overall straps inspired a farmer series. With shadowed face, their stance says "farmer". Seeing lace at an outdoor auction led to painting dark shadows to create a soft, sunlit feeling that recurs in my work. Magical moments with local children at parades resulted in another series.

I draw, paint, and draw again, using hatched lines and large washes to create depth.

Painting is a way to communicate and share my view of my world.

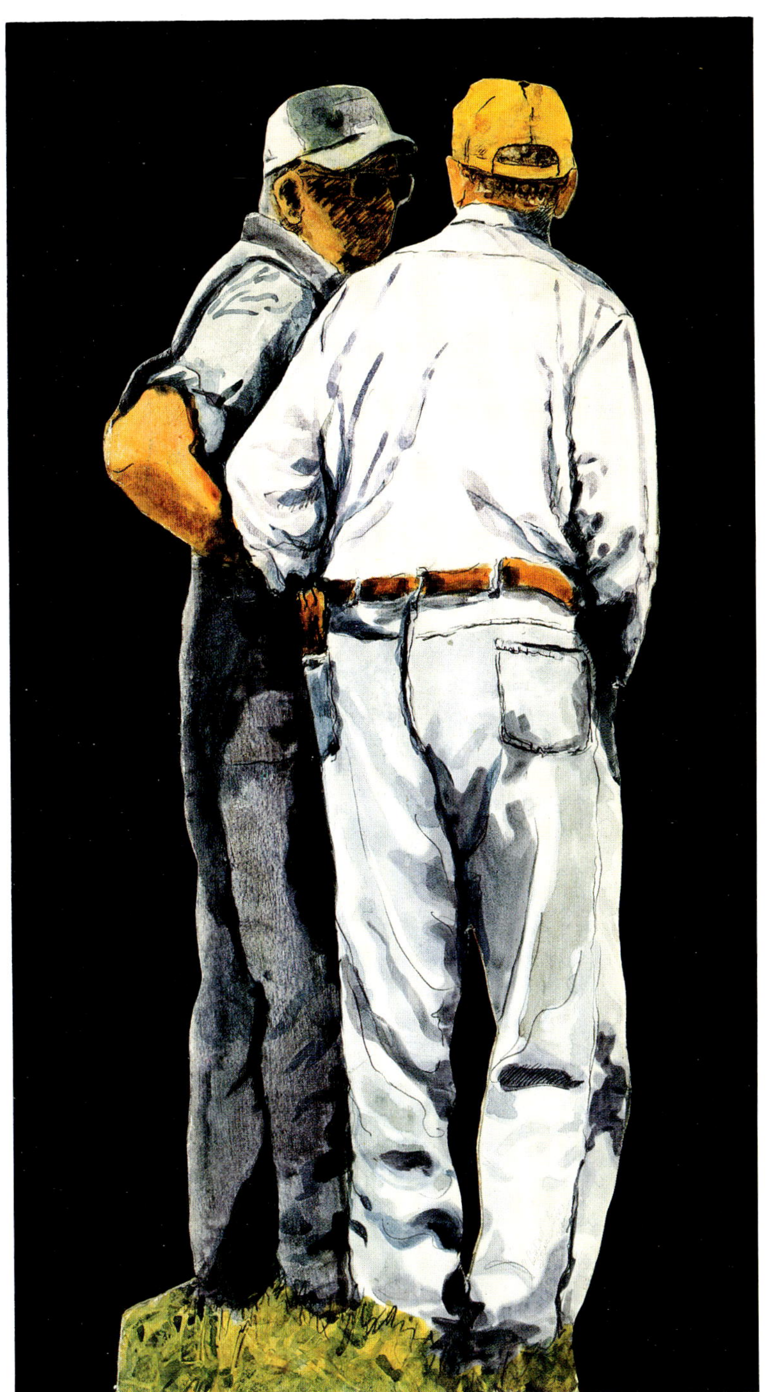

Standing Farmers   LaDell Routh Stonecipher, 38 x 16 in., watercolor cutout.

*I call my paintings "Prairie Horizons".
For me there is something special about
the place where the sky meets the earth…a
line sometimes clear and sharp,
sometimes so diffuse it melts into the
scene without leaving a trace.*

*I am a romantic and I want to portray the
vast expanse of the land and space.*

*I am also very interested in the patterns
of the land which I see in three levels: the
natural patterns of hills, trees, rivers and
clouds; the human-made patterns of
fences, roads and shapes of fields, and the
patterns of sunlight and shadow.*

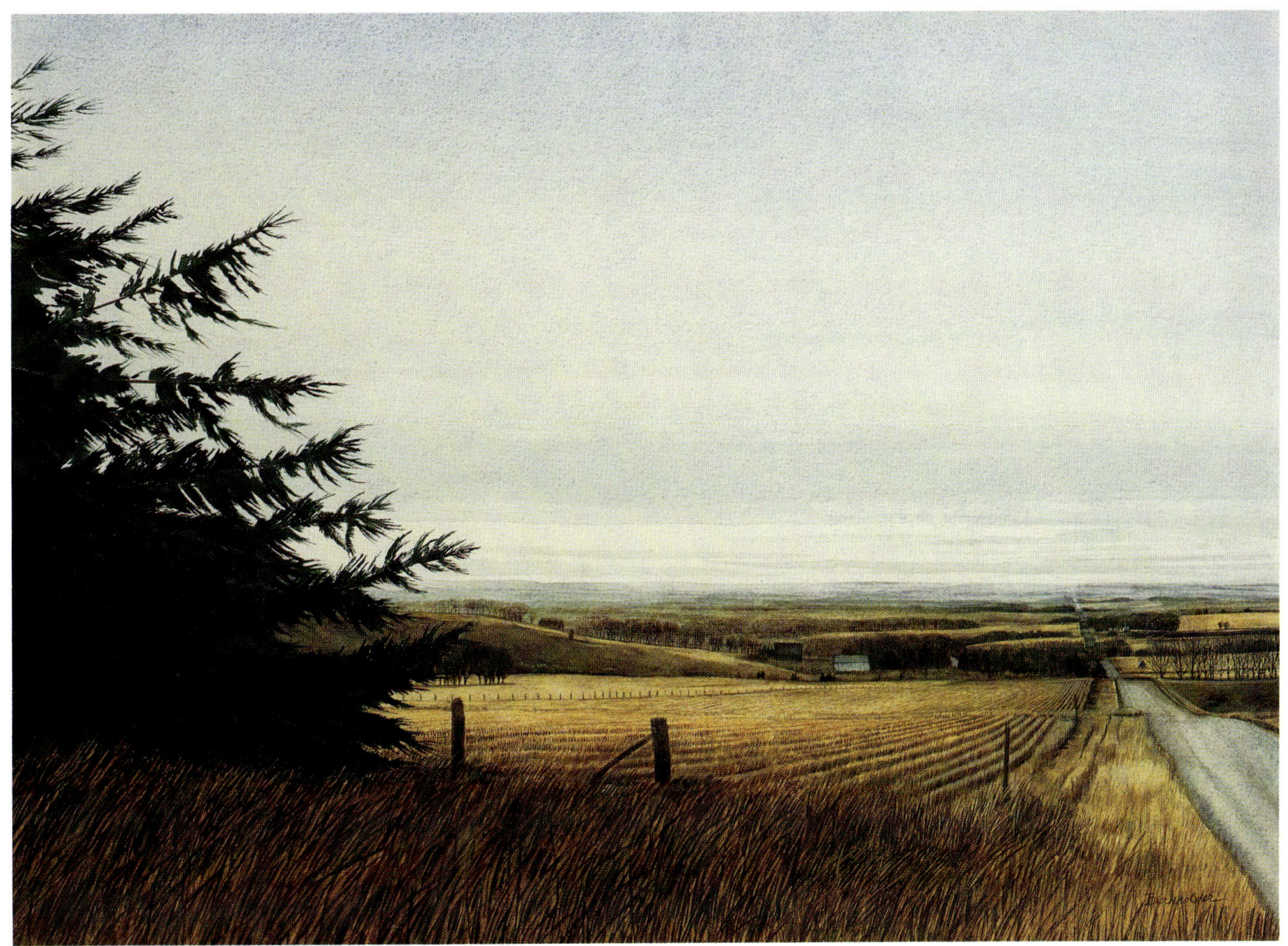

Horizon Otoe County Road   Anne Burkholder, 22 x 30 in., watercolor.

*The surface becomes
a global, visual
project and it
challenges my
beliefs, knowledge,
ability, awareness
and craftsmanship.*

*I try to inwardly
touch the viewer and
simultaneously, to
feel comfortable and
to be confident this is
my best for now -
then always
tomorrow, a better
work - there is no
end.*

*Regardless of the
subject or theme
selected, each
attempt is a degree
of abstraction and
construction.*

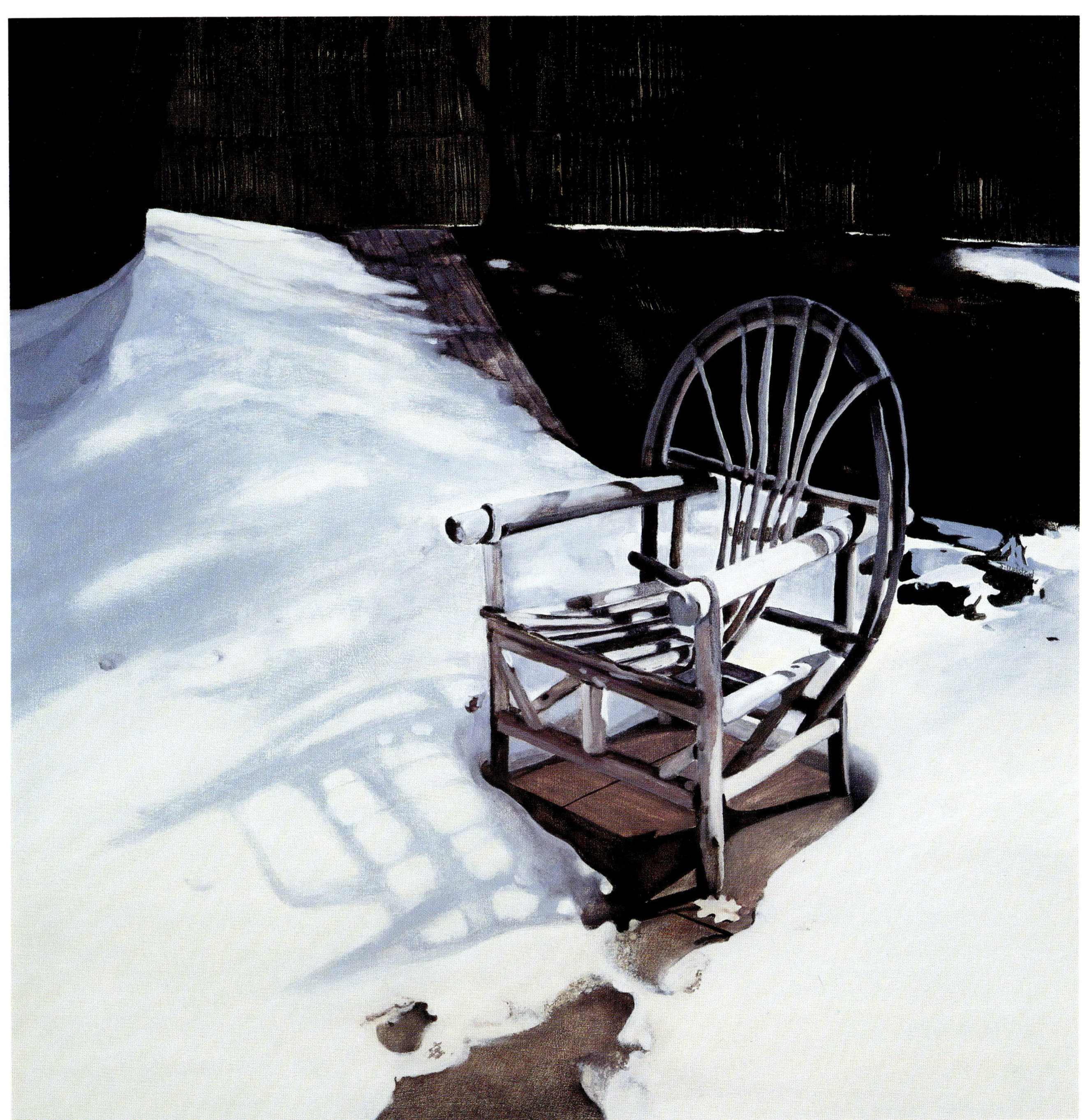

32 and Holding   Jean M. Welstead, 34 x 34 in., oil. Collection of FirsTier Bank, Lincoln.

Japanese screens, books of wood block prints with accordian folds
Rough paper - tactile, textural, visual
Transparent paint - opaque paint, one next to the other - pleasing

Still life imagery, patterned fabric, plants, flowers
Color, patterns, images
Images of colored patterns, plants, flowers, cloth
Relationships of patterns of color in paint on paper
Puzzle piece - fit together

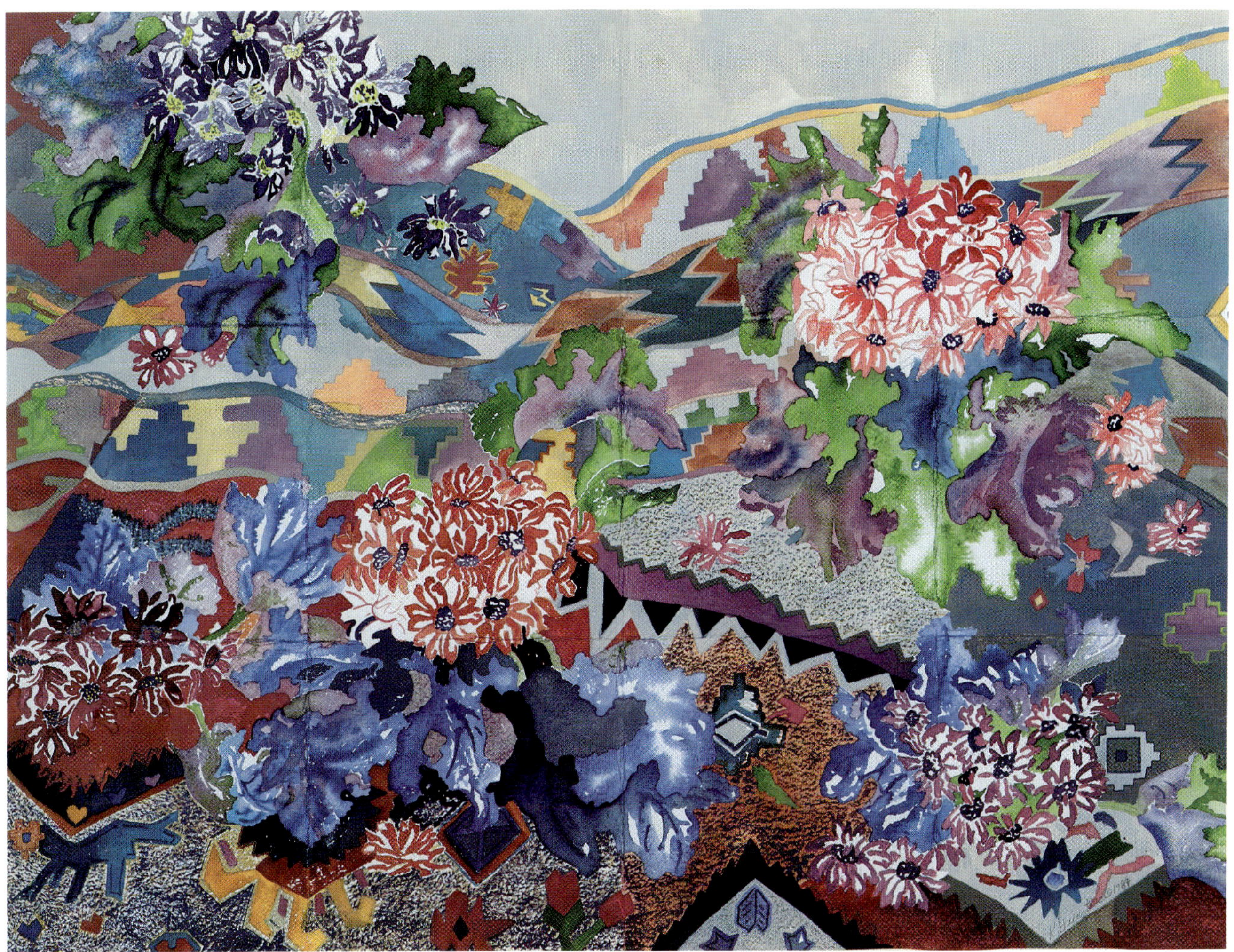

Turkish Tapestry III   Karen Dienstbier, 22 x 30 in., gouache, watercolor.

Even as a small child
* I knew I wanted to be an artist.*

As I grew older, I realized my obsession
* was with translating life into personal, visual terms.*

I am drawn to rural people and cultures.
* There I can best examine internal connections*
* with subject matter that address the rich complexity*
* of the human experience.*

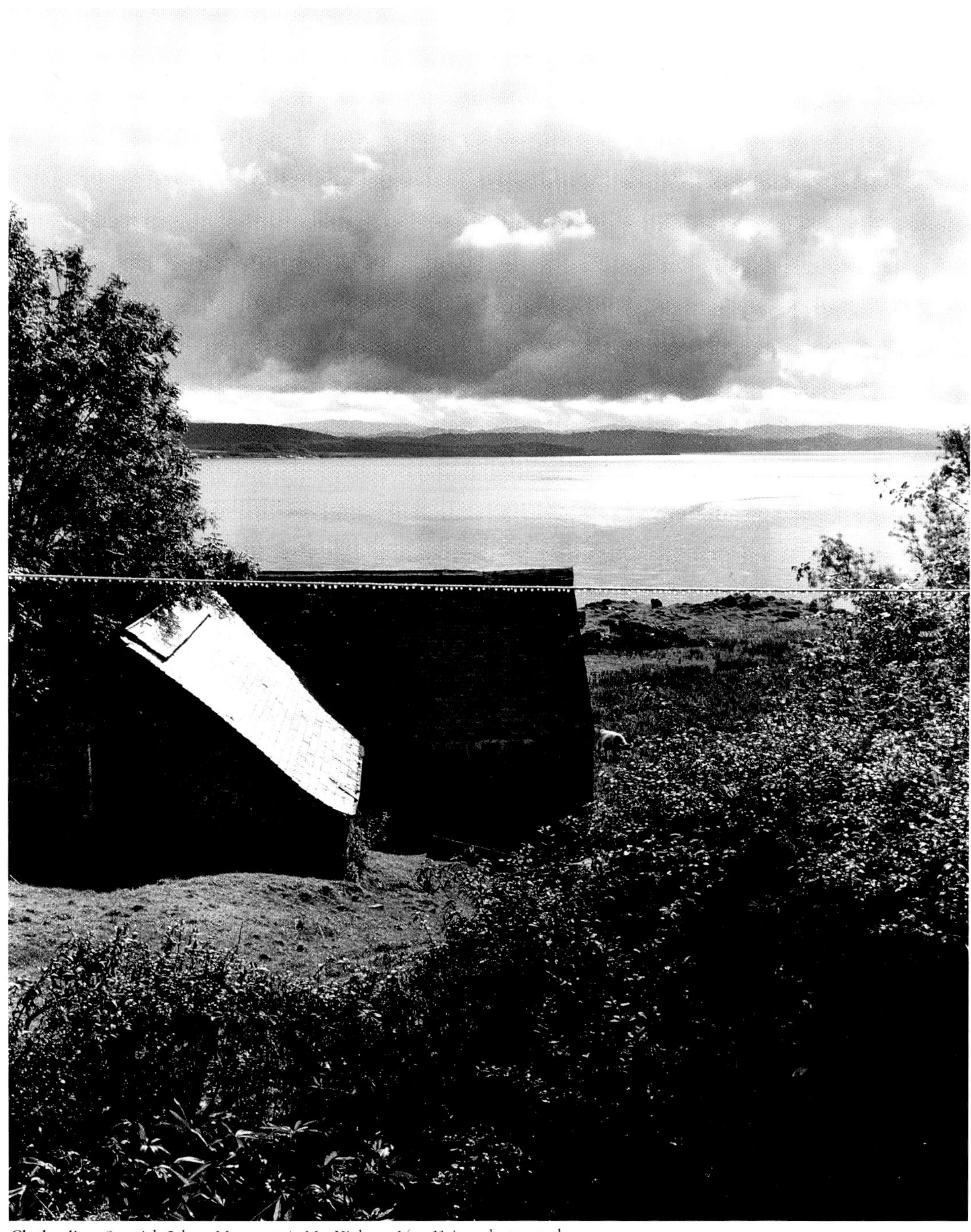

Clothesline, Scottish Isle   Margaret A. MacKichan, 14 x 11 in., photograph.

Contemporary music, fashion and way of life influence my style. Though I have worked a great deal with abstraction, I am experiencing an introspective phase which has evolved into a series of self portraits. Attending a mountain workshop, I found myself transfixed by the natural beauty and painting mountains, birds and trees which I later incorporated into my work. The painting in this exhibit evolved from this period.

Usually I rely primarily on sensory, especially visual, memory for inspiration. I try to balance spontaneity with intuition of technical knowledge. Color strengthens line, form and shape. Velocity and intensity propel my mental images onto my media.

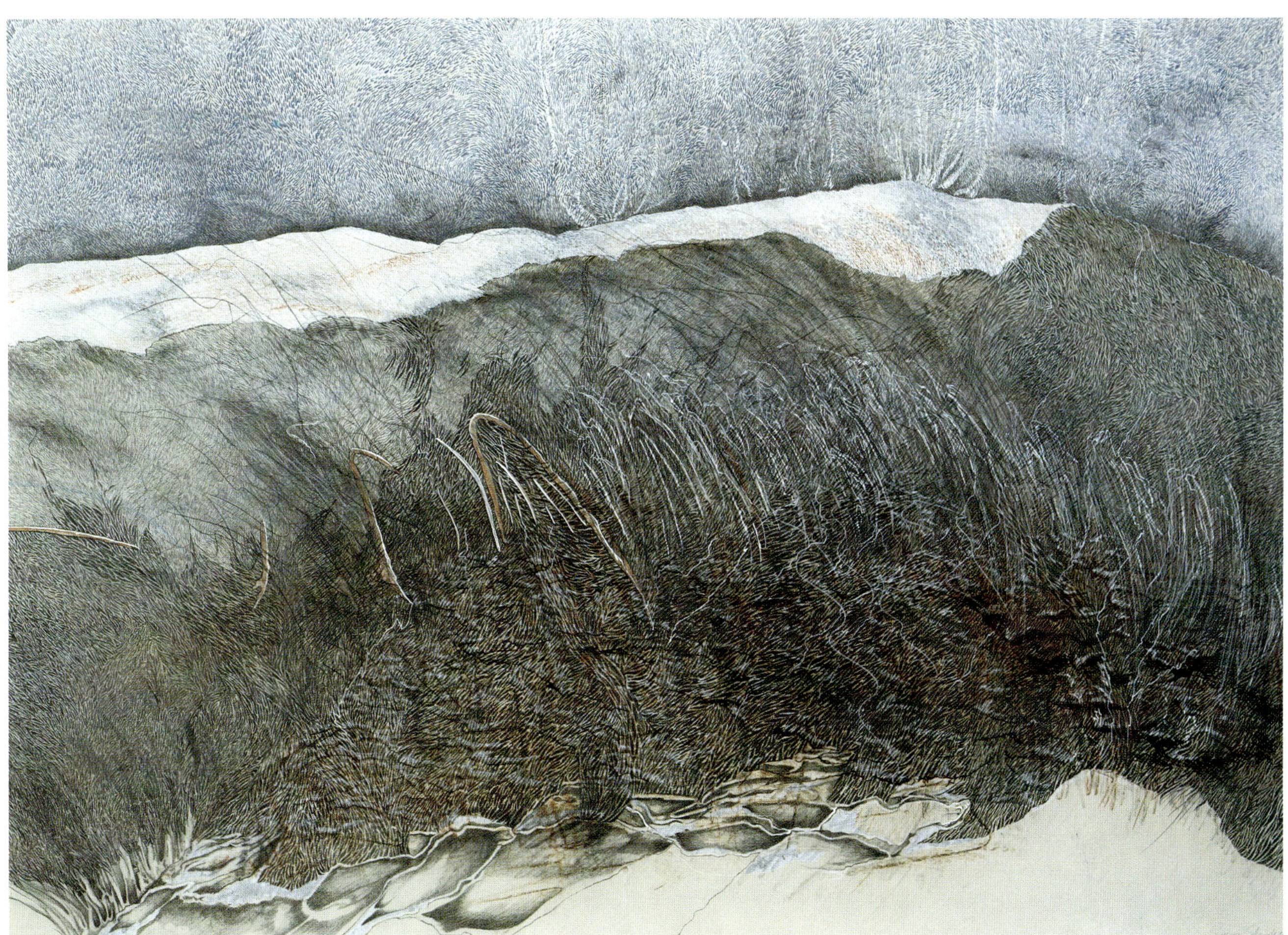

First Sweep Ridges, Then Plow   Mary Shindell, 30 x 44 in., mixed media, drawing.

Upon discovering that I am an artist, people often ask, "What's your medium?"
Instead of the typical response, "Watercolor or printmaking," I answer, "Color and texture.

I will use anything I can get my hands on to explore ways of working with color and texture: hand-made paper, packing papers (picked up from the street), trimming strips from a paper company, etc.

I use a variety of paints, ranging from tempera to interference metallics, to brush, roll and stain papers.

The collage process allows me to puzzle together the pieces and processes of the world that catch my eye: old, new, manufactured or found.

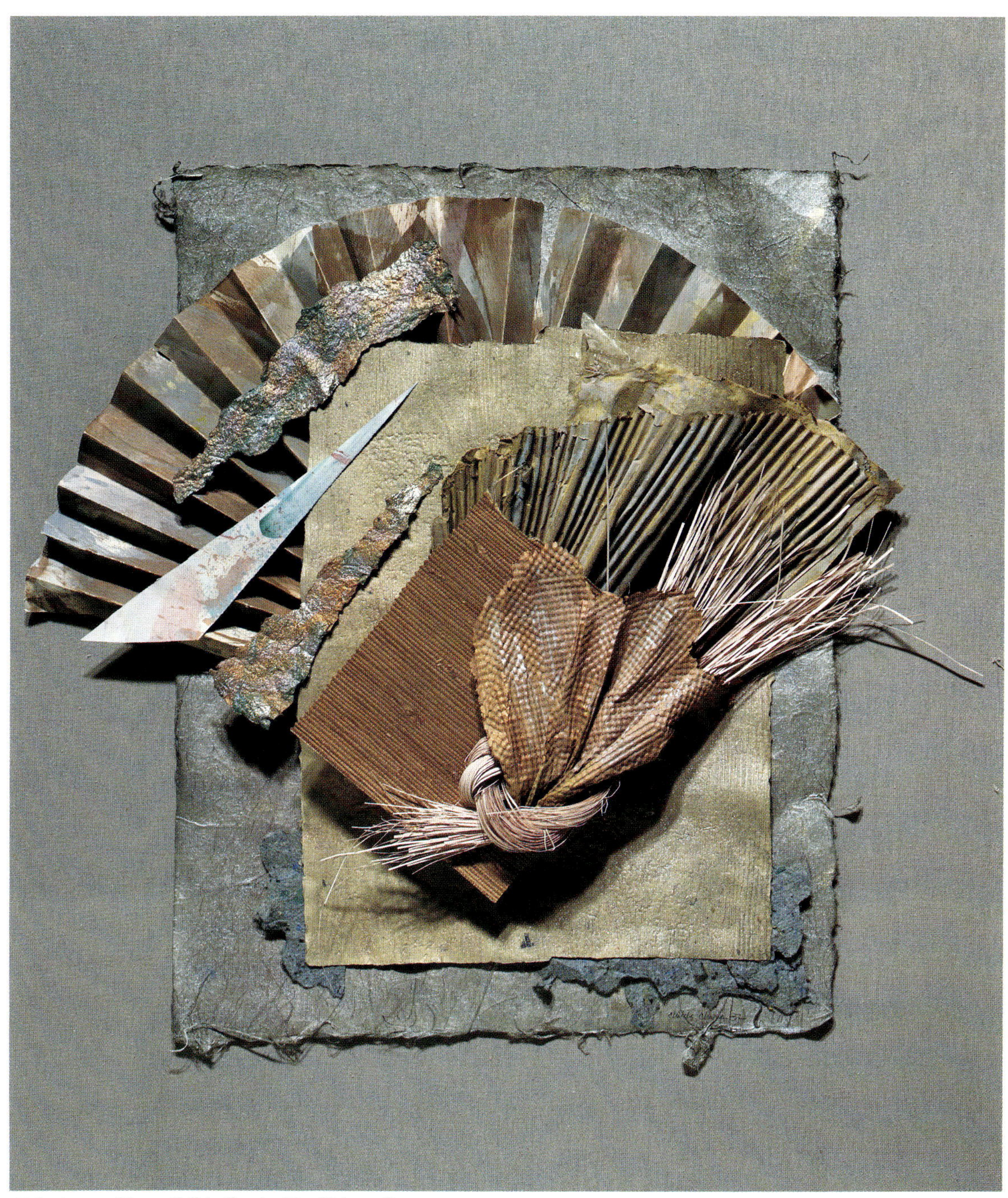

Cielo Azuro   Nancy Childs Chapin, 24 x 25 in., collage.

I am captivated by the intensity of sunlight.
The resulting lacework of shadow,
luminous in its contrast,
invites exploration.
I love sifting through the potential of a subject,
reaching for new design possibilities,
looking deeper than the surface.
I want the best I can achieve.
I am very interested in color relationships
and the power of design.

Art puts a creative energy into my life.
It is an ongoing relationship I cherish.
It's a personal challenge with no ending
and I am reminded of a quote by Karen Raven,

"Only as high as I reach can I grow."

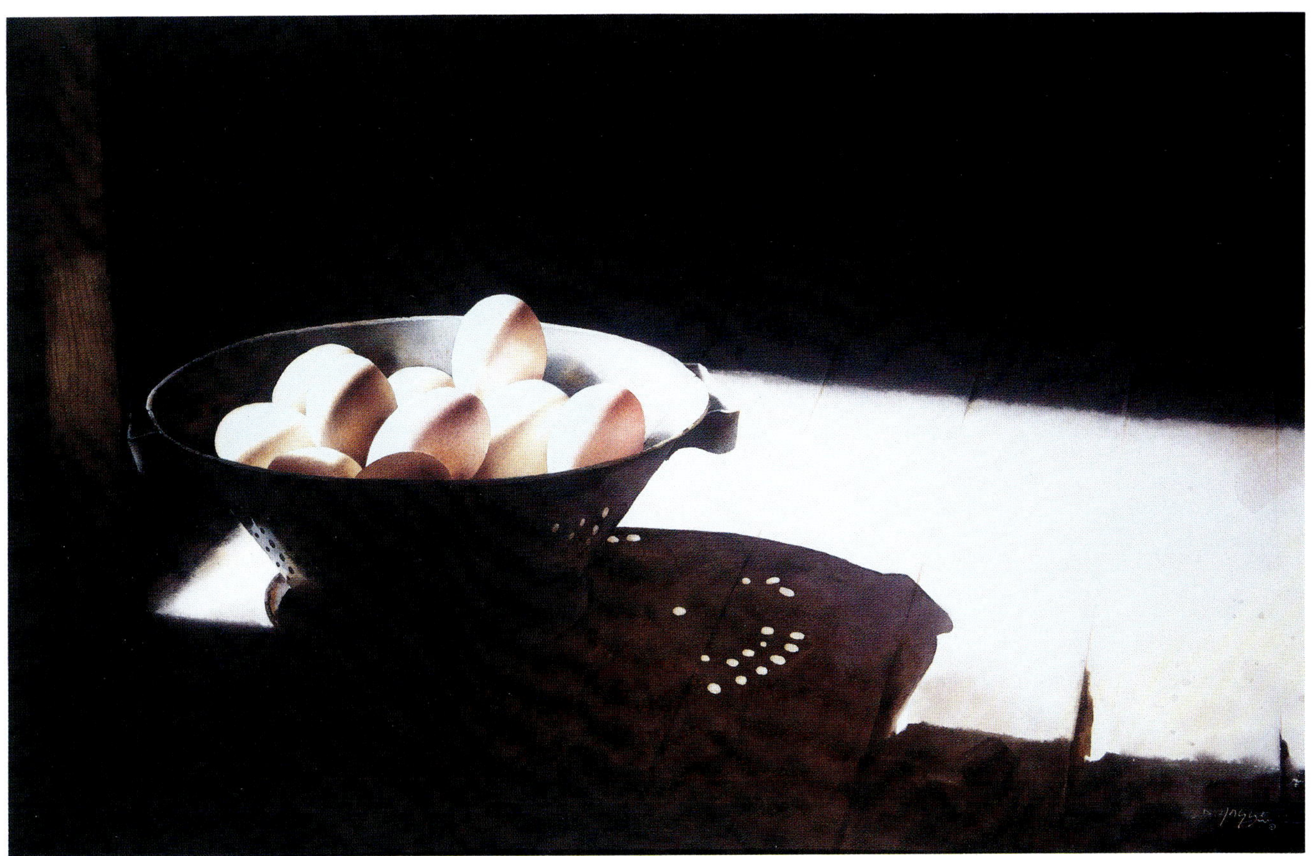

Simplism of Light   Dora Hagge, 19 x 31 in., watercolor.

First, my subject confronts me. It may be a house or building that I have seen thousands of times, or only once. It catches my attention; its structure, its detail, the way sunlight and shadows play upon it.

Then -

I confront it. It is really a big history book. I think of the people who must have once inhabited it, the clothes that they wore, the things that they did. I picture it in my acrylic paints and think, "If walls could talk..."

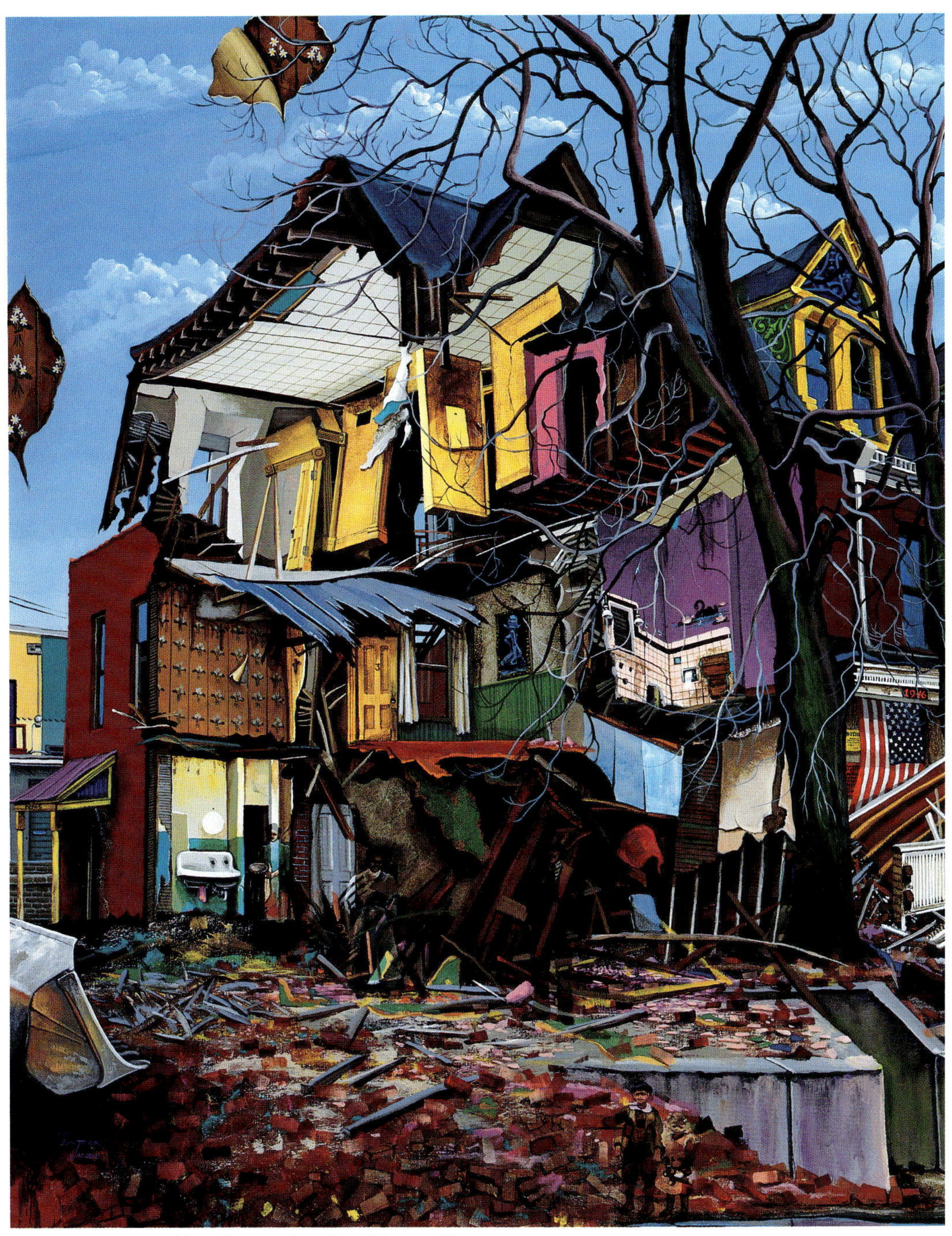

Demolition Day   Bobbi Baltzer-Jacobo, 40 x 32 in., acrylic on canvas.

My work reflects a lifelong love of natural forms and textures. However, I use them only as a starting point to allow my feelings to capture the essence of a sense.

Sometimes I start drawing with only a few shapes or forms suggested in pencil. Then imagination and intuition take over as it grows on the sheet of paper. I stop when it feels complete and right.

I find that translating a drawing into the reverse image of a woodcut can create beautiful and dramatic results. Sometimes I use the natural grain of my woodcut boards to impart the feeling I am striving for.

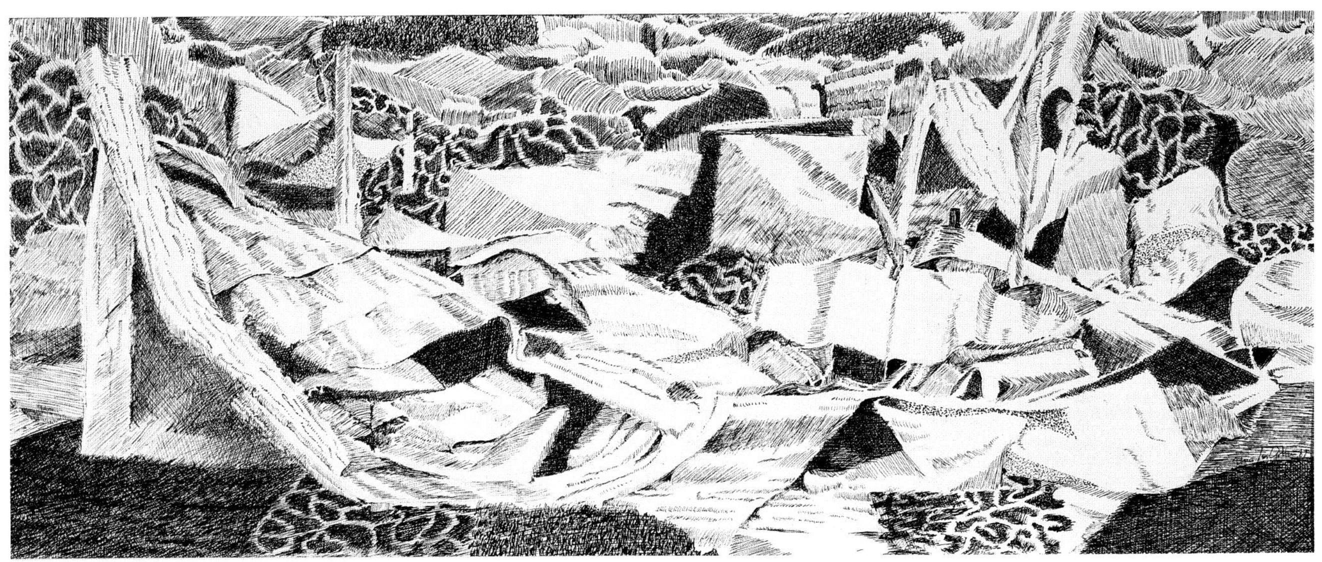

Tangled Web   Dona Lee Golden, 30 x 16 in., pen and ink drawing.

Early morning and late afternoon sunlight playing on objects is often the initial inspiration for my paintings. Each layer of color connects subject to shadow, reflection to illusion.

Painting to classical music helps me achieve the lyrical sense I'm after and helps me define the color schemes and direction of each passage throughout a painting.

Glorified by light, shadow and reflection, I combine garden flowers, fabrics and various collected items such as cicada wings, shark teeth or shells to create compositions with emotional and psychological intrigue. I wish to share my joy in "seeing" common objects in our everyday world.

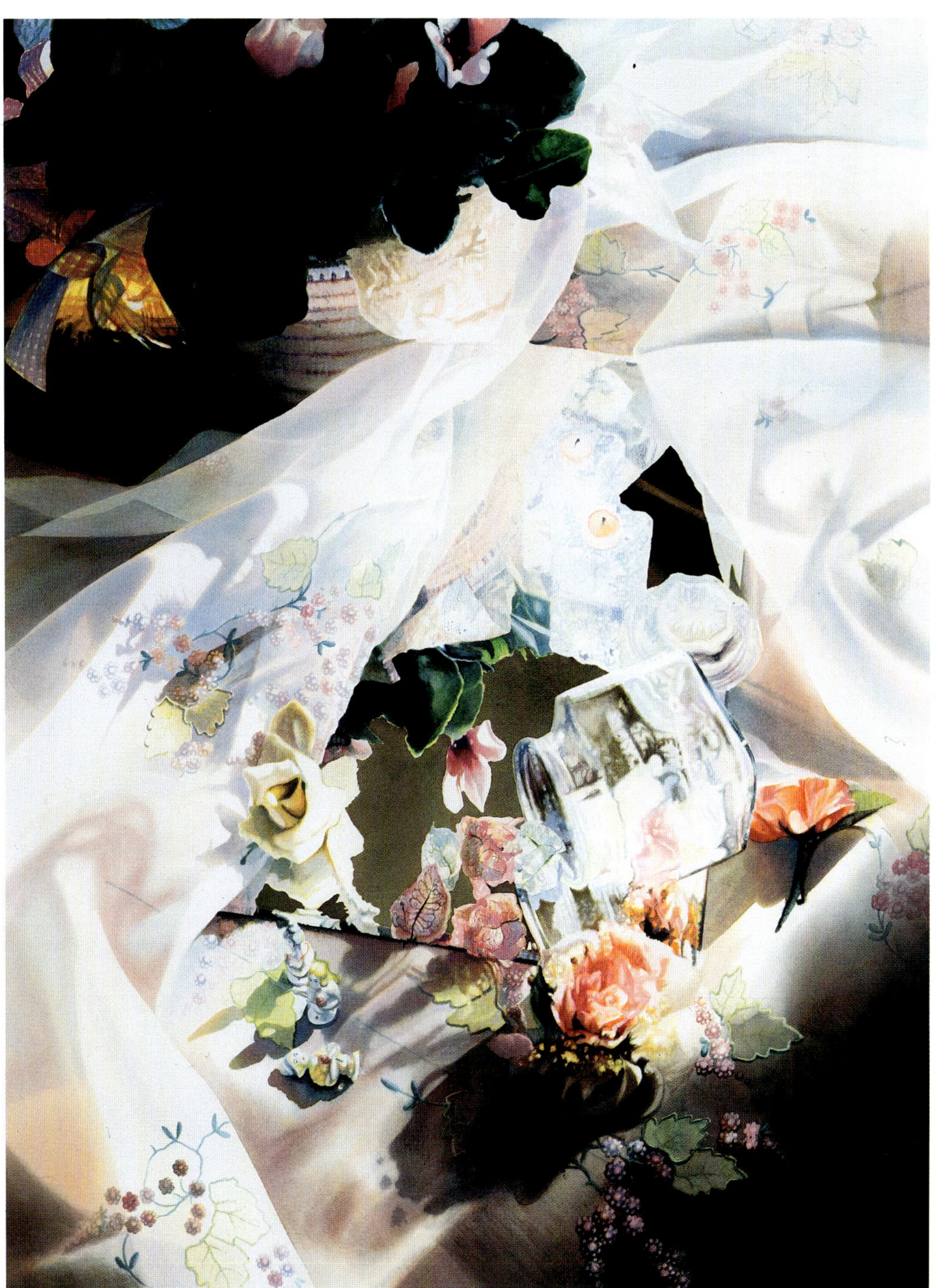

Still Life With Jar And Dried Bougainvillea   Sue Olson-Mandler, 40 x 30 in., transparent watercolor.

Art is a vehicle through which my inner experiences, such as dreams, insights and intuition are manifested on a physical level. It is the essence of these experiences that I translate into clay. The result of this process uplifts the consciousness.

I work toward strengthening my relationship with the creative force, understanding its ways and establishing a greater harmony with it.

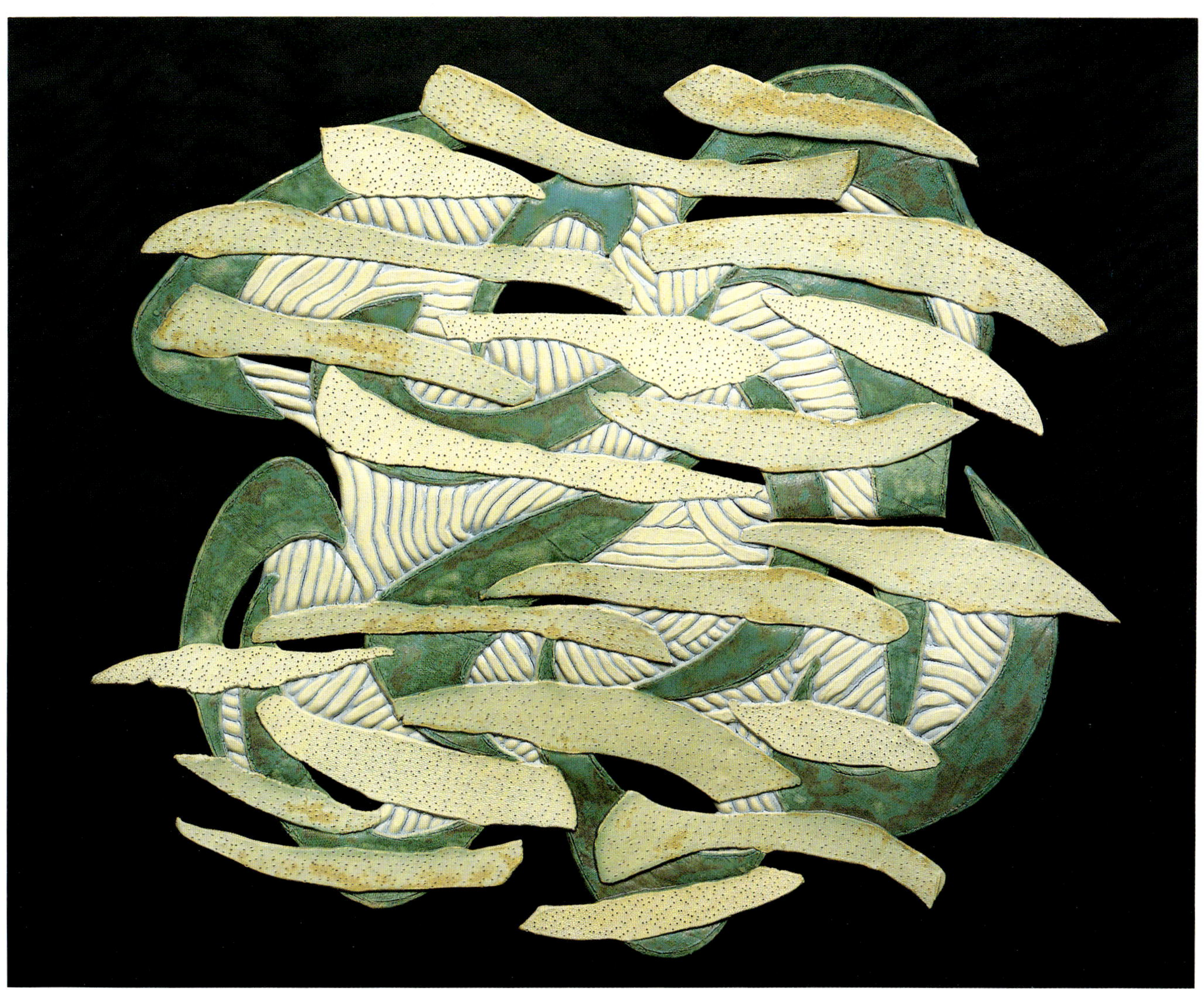

Suspended In The Sound   Lynelle Youngquist, 19 x 23 in., ceramic.

*E*ach canvas is a challenge:
I strive to bring all the elements of color
and design into a cohesive painting, a
painting which satisfies me as an artist
and also pleases the viewer.

*W*hile color is of primary importance to me,
I try to maintain a good balance between
color and composition. I am, at heart, a
hardedge painter and prefer my paintings
sharply defined as I interpret the play of
light and shadow on surfaces and the
resulting shapes of color.

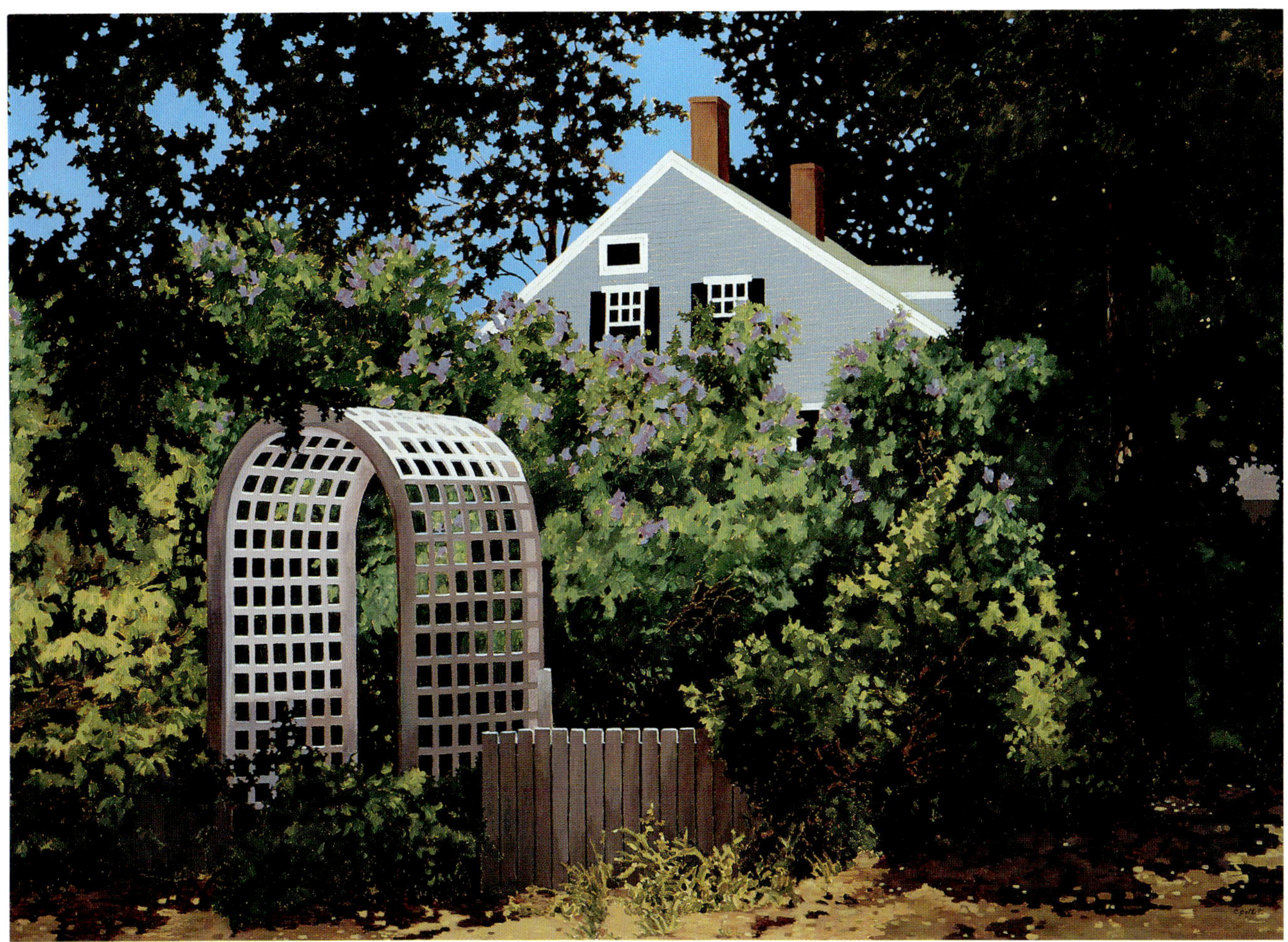

Lilac Time   Carol Pettit, 42 x 60 in., oil.

I work back and forth between realism and abstraction, turning first outward and then inward. The intense absorption in the subject matter that realism, especially life drawing, demands is balanced by a personal symbolism in my abstract art.

For me, abstract paintings are far more difficult. They are from a confusing realm in which a metallic disc, a scratched, tormented gesso or a jewel-like color emerging from the darkness have their own wordless meanings.

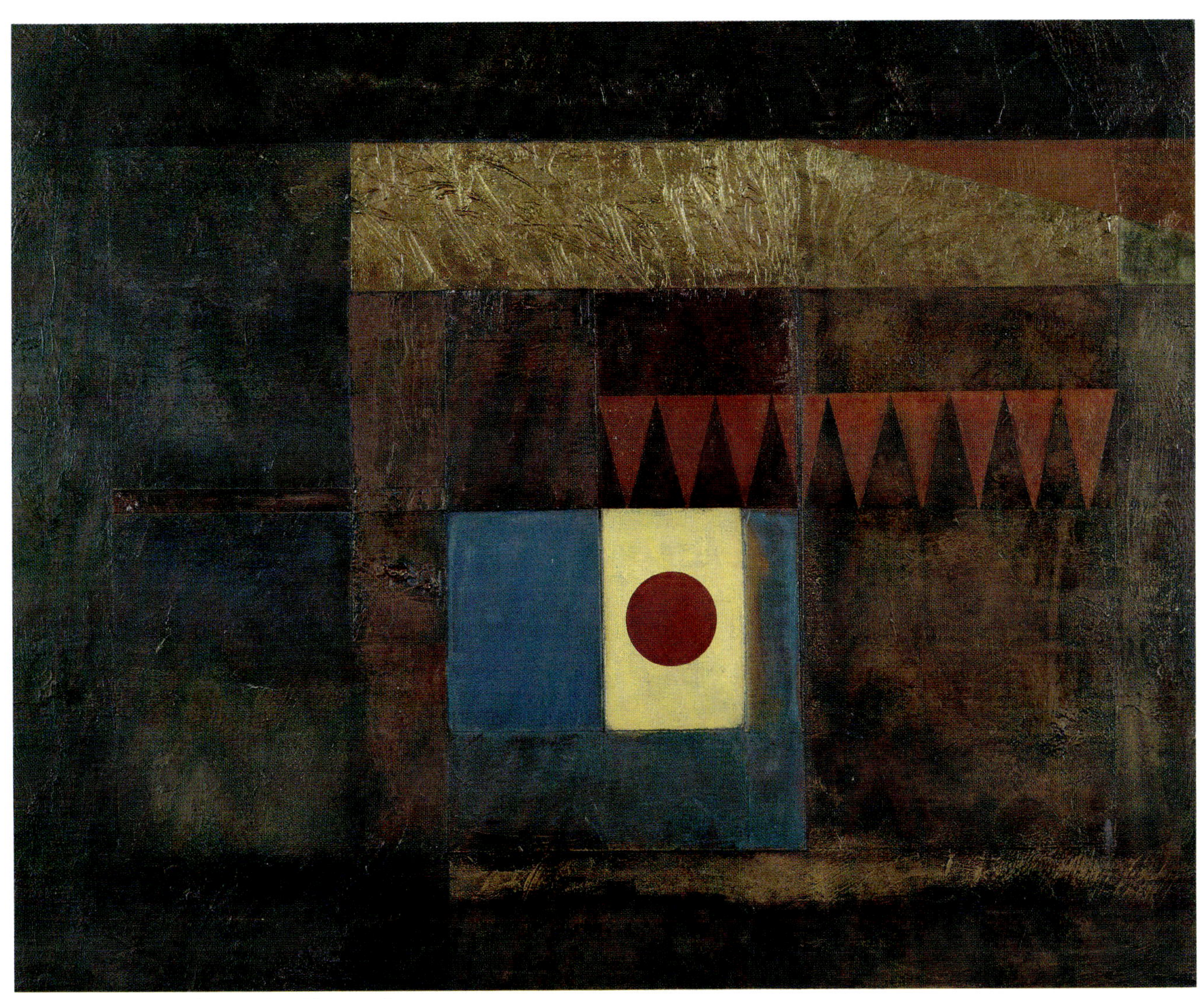

Pavilion   Michele Angle Farrar, 30 x 24 in., acrylic.

*The intent of my sculpture is not
necessarily to fool the eye into believing
'this is real',
but more to gently surprise the viewer
with the hard facts of life, softened.*

*Manipulation of the flat batik design
with needle and thread to become a
quilted wall hanging or sculpture is an
extension of the energy involved in batik.
It also allows the fabric to catch and add
light and shadow to the work.*

*Realistically representing the subject
with personal emotion and humor help
keep me from taking myself
too seriously.*

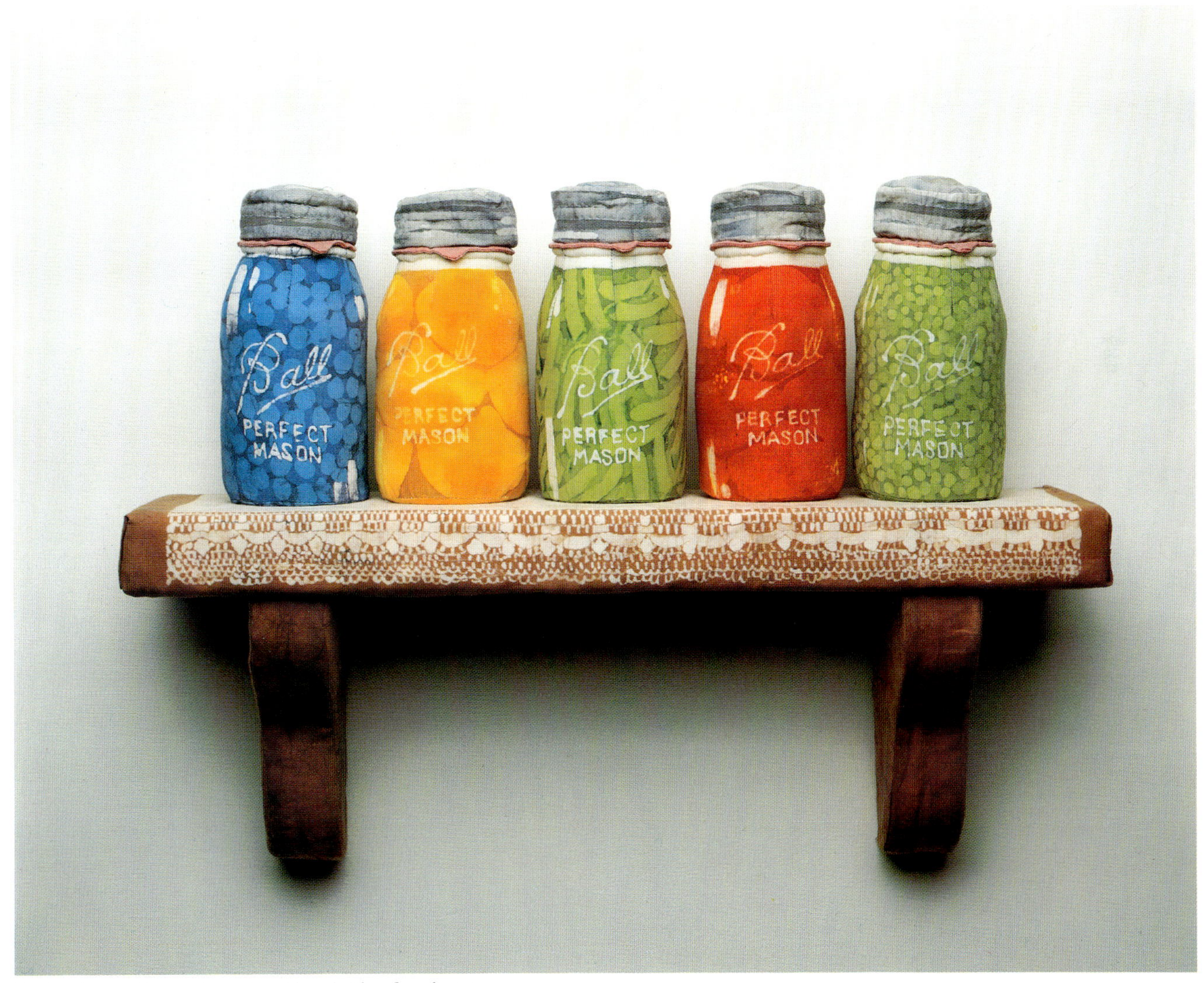

Kitchen Shelf   Sammy Lynn, 17 x 24 in., batik soft sculpture.

Every glimpse, every experience adds to a visual literacy which deepens with time and memory - all the fragments intertwine in the subconscious to be pieced together later in paint.

While painting, my mind goes into automatic pilot developing an intensity which peaks out after the struggle, and when a painting is done - I know it's done. Knowing when to stop is as important as starting. Scrubbing the surface of many layers gets at the essence of the form and idea.

Painting has a life of its own that starts with an idea, then evolves with the physical contact of paint on surface - I'm always surprised at this process.

Green Bay Sue Devlin, 48 x 72 in., acrylic and chalk.

*T*here is a private part of me which seldom finds a sounding board.

It is the search . . . arrival . . . and departure of an unrelenting passion called creativity. For me, the subject is simply a tool to set the mood. Woodcut, ancient and earthy, enchants me, perhaps because the knife slicing the wood leaves such a defined edge. I love challenging that unyielding mark by breaking the old rules, using unorthodox color methods, distorting perspective, interspersing disassociated objects and mixing media.

Using this nonverbal voice, I seek to touch a cord of inner vision and challenge the viewer to see the unexpected.

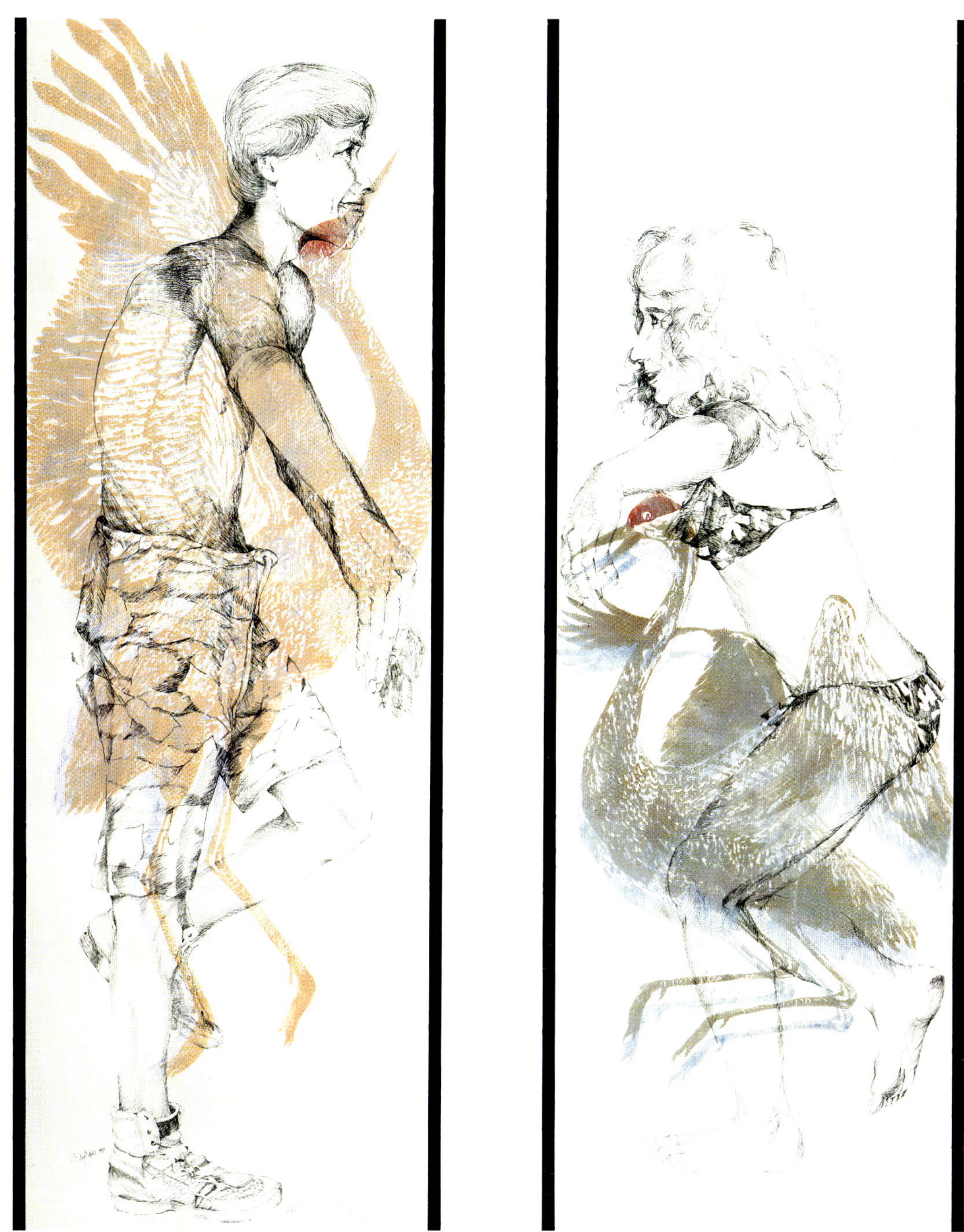

Nebraska Courtship Amy A. Sadle, 60 x 20 in. each, woodcut, ink, edition.

*For me, the remembrance of a place and
the circumstances of a real location, or
instant in time, combined and invented
in the studio are starting points.*

*The whole picture is barely glimpsed,
told in parts — like seeing a bird in flight
through dense trees - because you
happened to look up!*

*But I've set myself up for this creative
occurence - by looking, being alert,
knowing what has happened before, and
what could happen - like
being out walking!*

*Each walk creates another chance, and I
might be lucky enough to actually catch
that view! The images are the
unpredictable phenomenon of what
happens while I work and what I
decide to do next.*

*It is like the weather - combinations of
air, land, movements, - ambiguous -
endlessly variable - and sometimes
wonderful.*

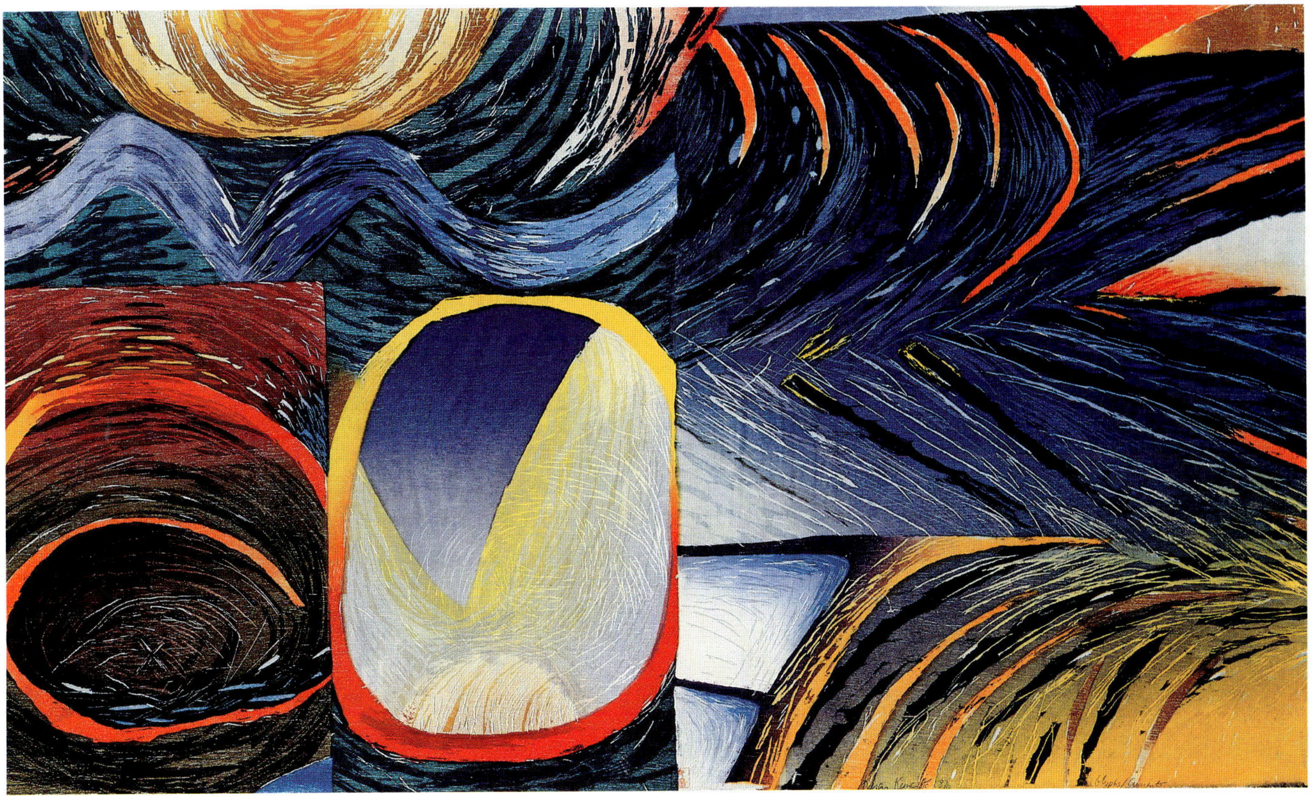

Glyphs/Currents Karen Kunc, 24 x 41 in., woodcut.

Ecru lace and chrome,
organdy slips and black lacquer boxes.
A midsummer night's dream,
gold scarab amulets, luna chrysalis, a chambered nautilus.
Orion's belt, oriental patterns, red satin, glass hearts, grey silk.
Clove and vetiver, blood red tea roses.

Ethereal yet tangible…paradoxical images.
Time told in midnight blue rooms,
Time that fascinates…through a misted lens,
a personal view that isolates…enigma…
romance.

Silver slippers gliding across a moonlit marble floor,
Cole Porter, Billie Holliday, Fitzgerald, Marienbad.

The Chrysler Building at dusk,
Paris in the rain, a foggy London dawn.
Vienna, LaBelle Epoque…not today…
yesterdays…
sentimental journey.

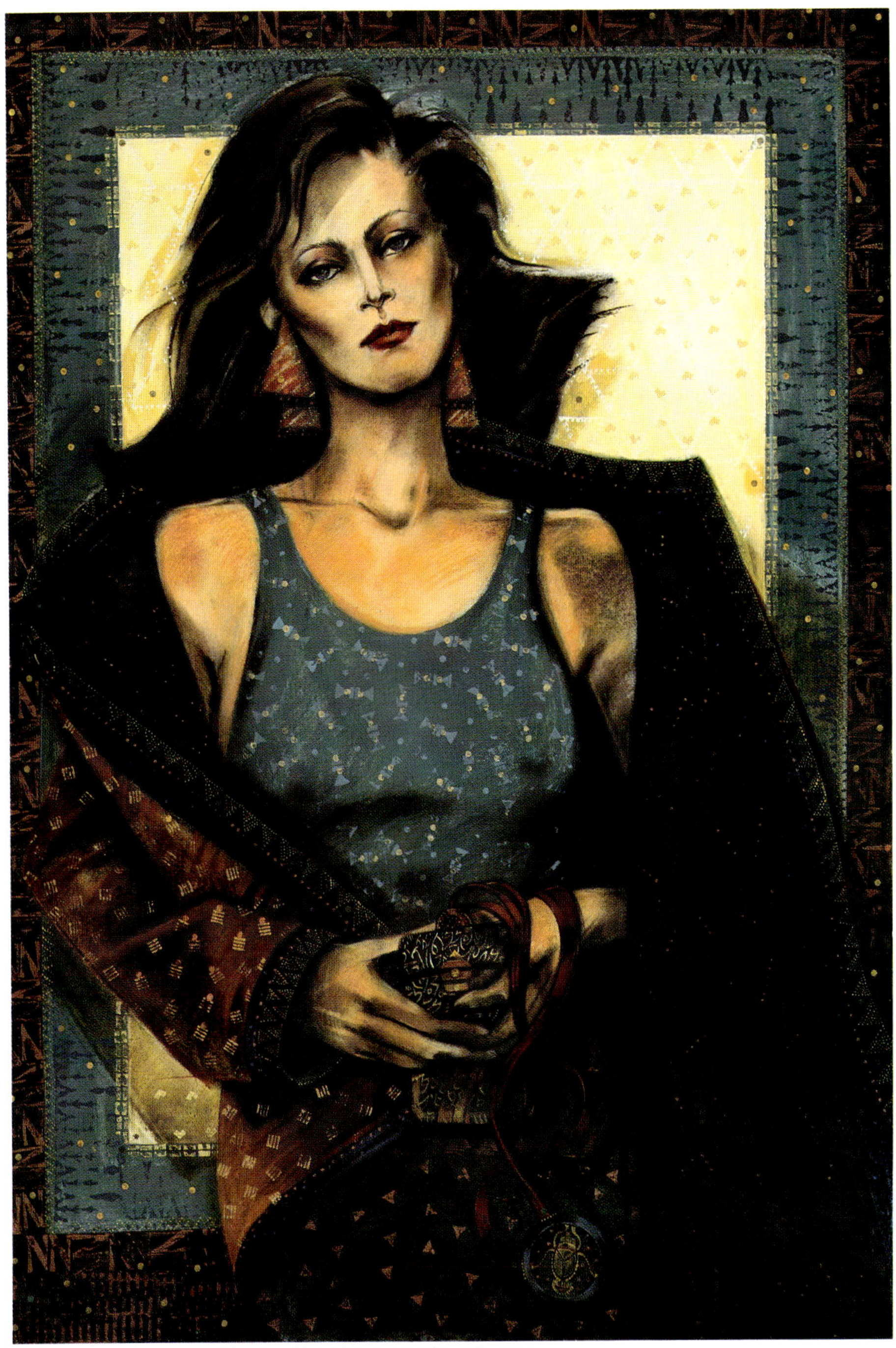

Vision of Shelia   Lynn Soloway, 50 x 34 in., mixed media.

There are so many magical moments created by the whimsical play of the young or the power of the challenges faced by those who are older. I want to capture that instant in my wood sculpture. I know I've caught it when I see a smile or hear a giggle as someone studies my work.

I love working with wood because the medium itself might have provided shelter or fed or even witnessed the turn of a timid head or watched the action and grace of an animal bidding a hasty retreat.

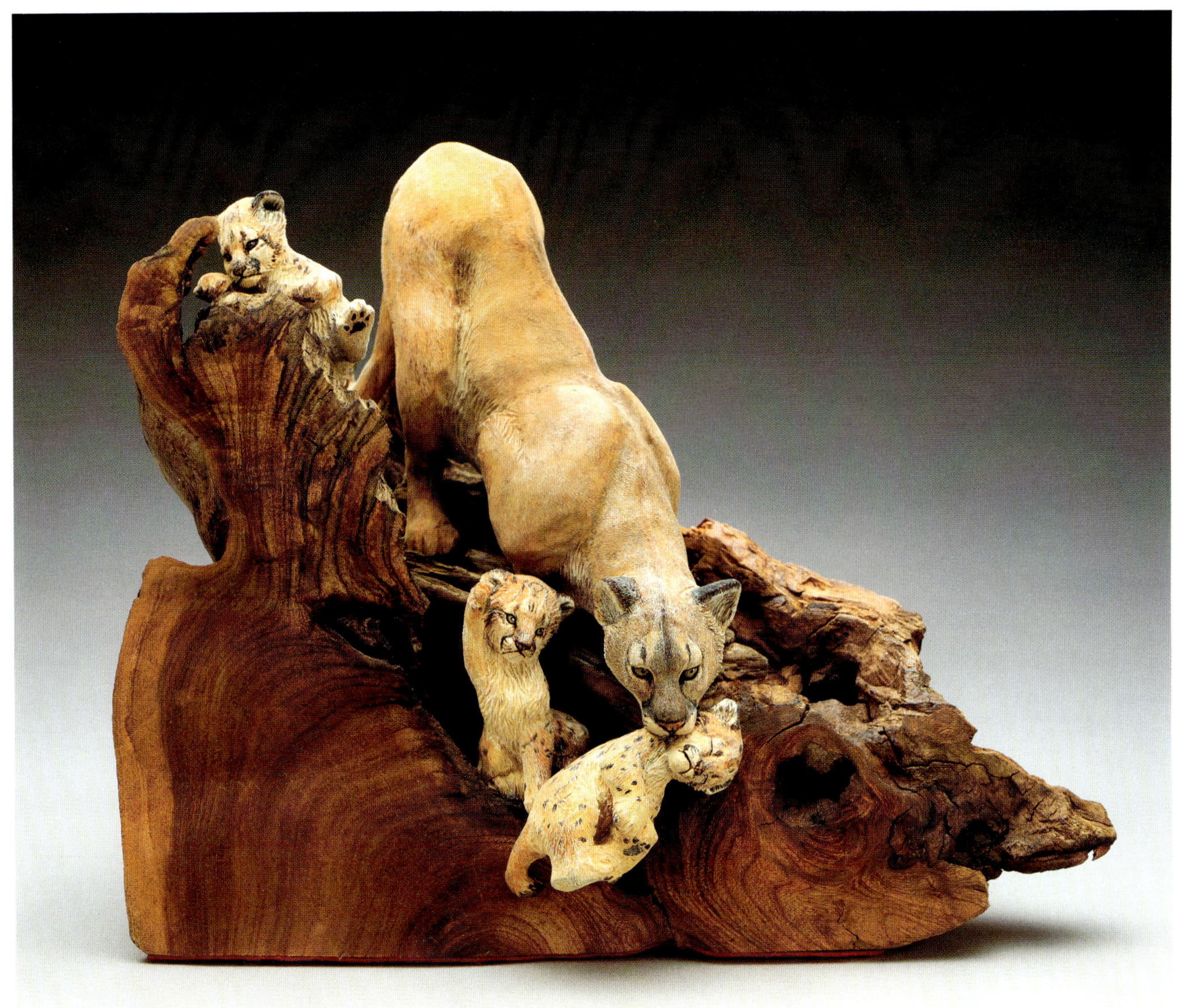

Movin' Problems   Desiree Hajny, 10 x 6 in., wood carving.

Landscapes are my primary subject matter. I may choose intimate segments or more comprehensive views, but it is the atmosphere and light that are the real subjects. I am especially drawn to the edges of day when light is more dramatic and colors and shadows deepen.

My painting is an emotional response to a part of nature caught in a moment of time. When I'm painting on site, all my senses are involved. My goal is to so involve viewers that they go beyond the visual and also feel the breeze, smell the clover or hear the rush of water.

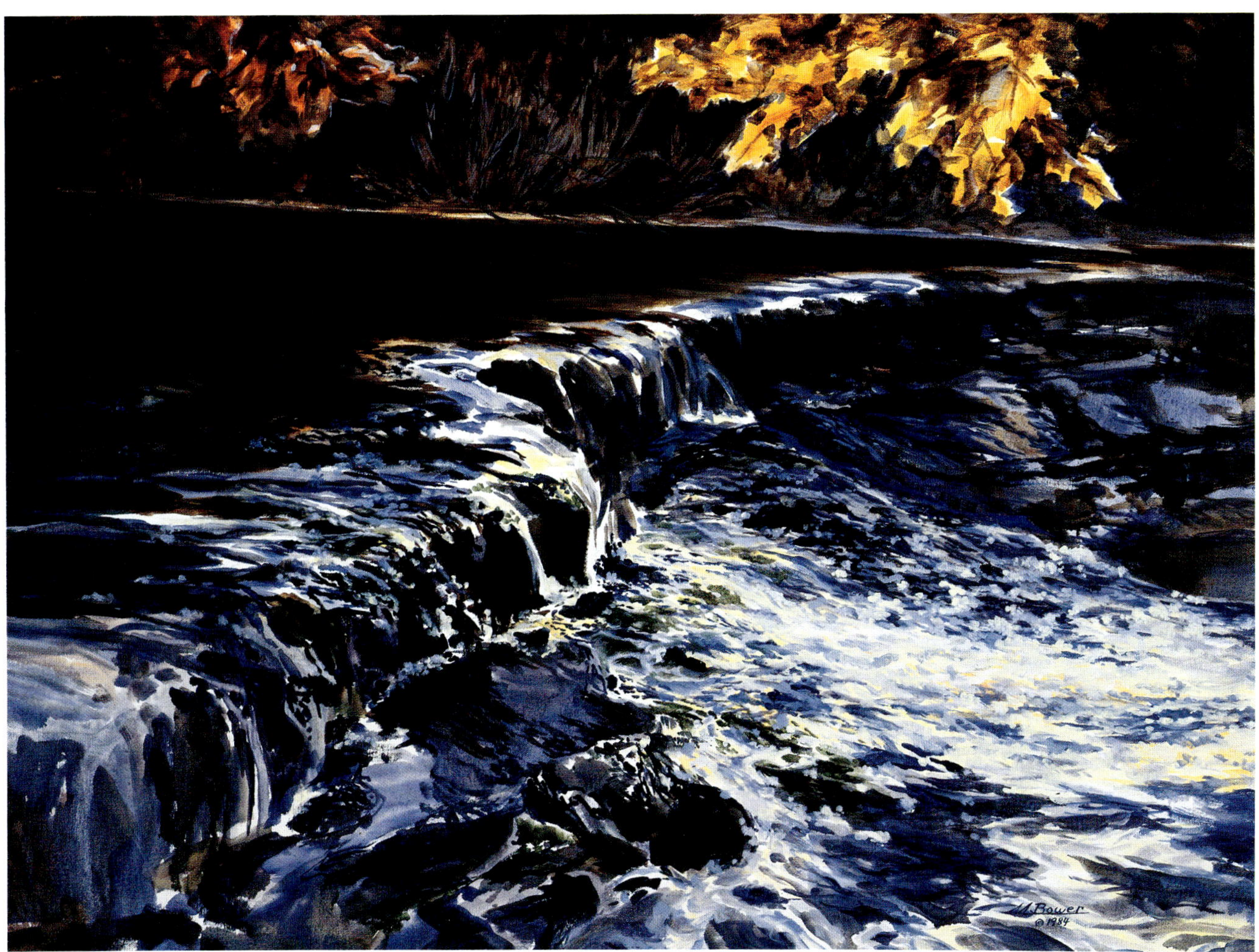

Clear and Cold   Marilyn Bower, 28 x 38 in., oil.

I'm intrigued with cast shadows and how they distort our view of life. This fascination, combined with images perceived through peripheral vision, is the inspiration for my art.

I rely on the play of strong lights and darks to set the foundation. The shapes of the objects, how they overlap or collide, build from the foundation and set up new tensions. Color adds to this, or may complement existing movement. Finally, middle values and detailing give intimacy. When I'm actively working on a painting, all this happens without conscious effort on my part.

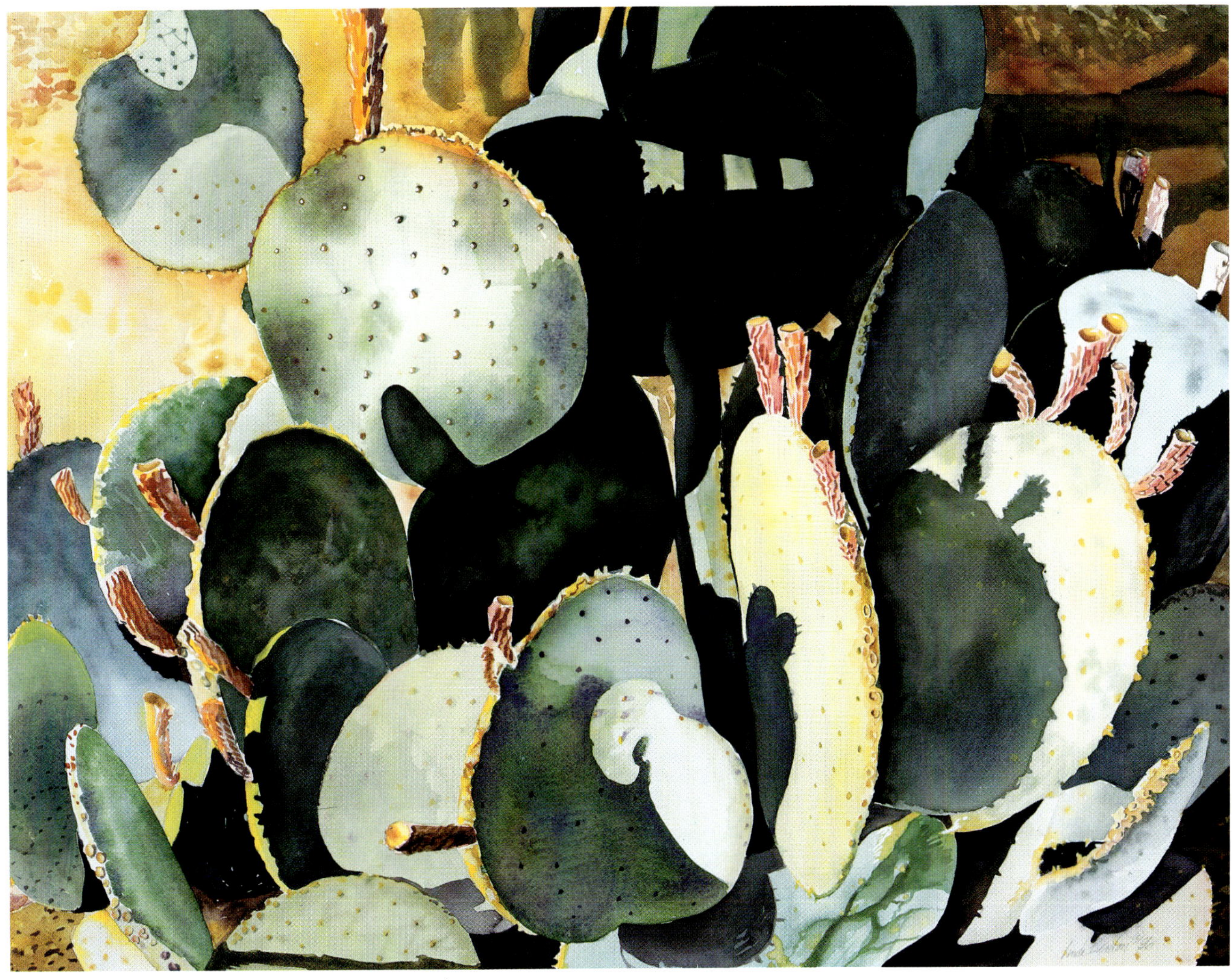

Masked Cactus   Linda K. Benton, 22 x 30 in., watercolor.

I am rarely without a pencil in my hand. Neither is my daily life disconnected for long from mental image making. Ideas flicker by like migratory birds . . . some stay longer than others and become drawings and paintings.

I hardly care at all about my paintings when they are finished. The painting of them is what makes me happy. When I see a painting I have sold, it doesn't seem familiar to me - sort of like a slight acquaintance.

I'm never really sure I'm finished with a painting. The work just seems to slow and I find I don't know what color to pick up next.

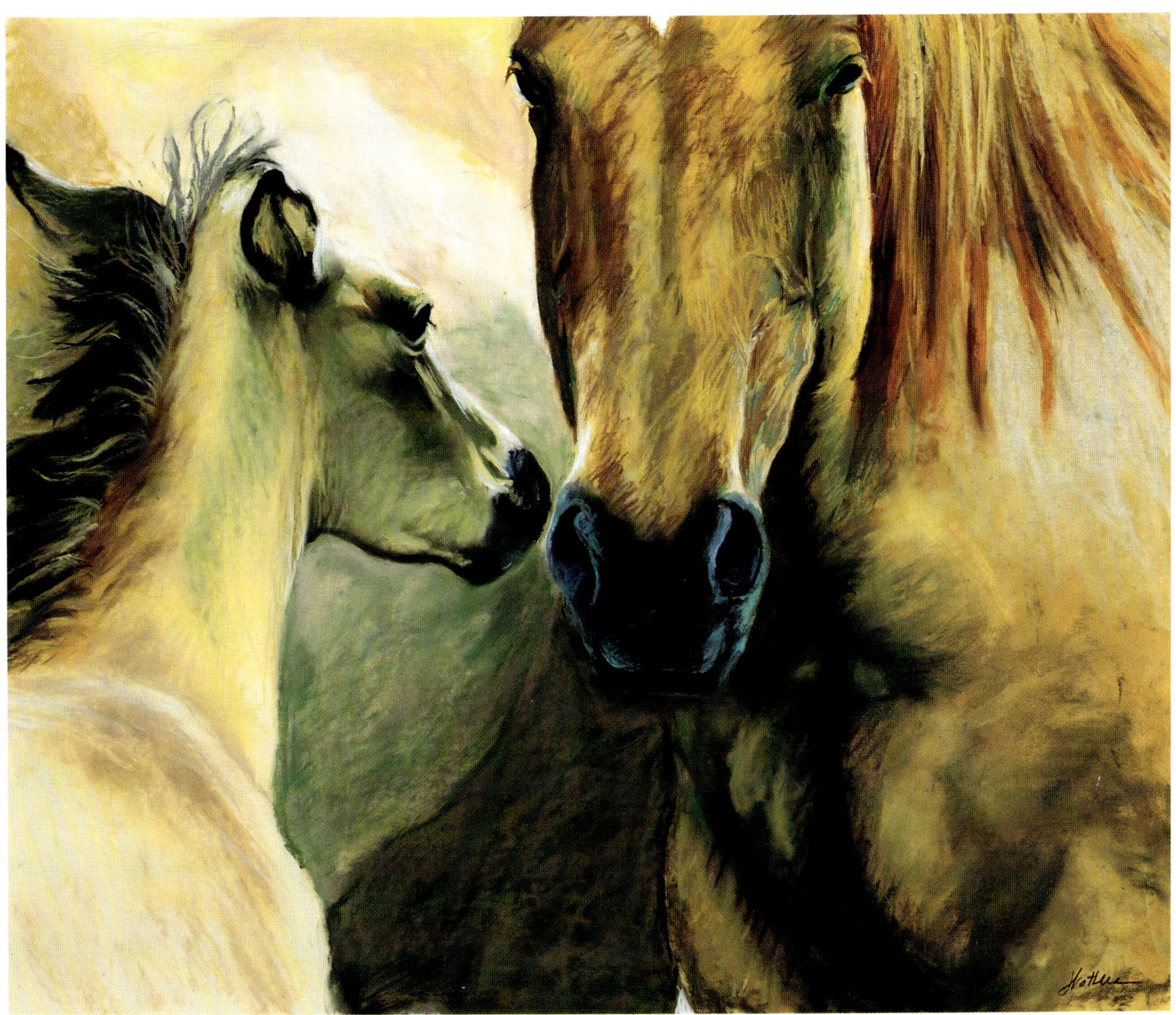

Taking Care Virginia Wattles, 25 x 30 in. pastel.

Making art is a way to express the inexpressible. I tend to be driven in this regard and have spent many years in my studio developing my work, drawing, painting and exploring sculptural materials. I'm striving to create an architecture for the human spirit.

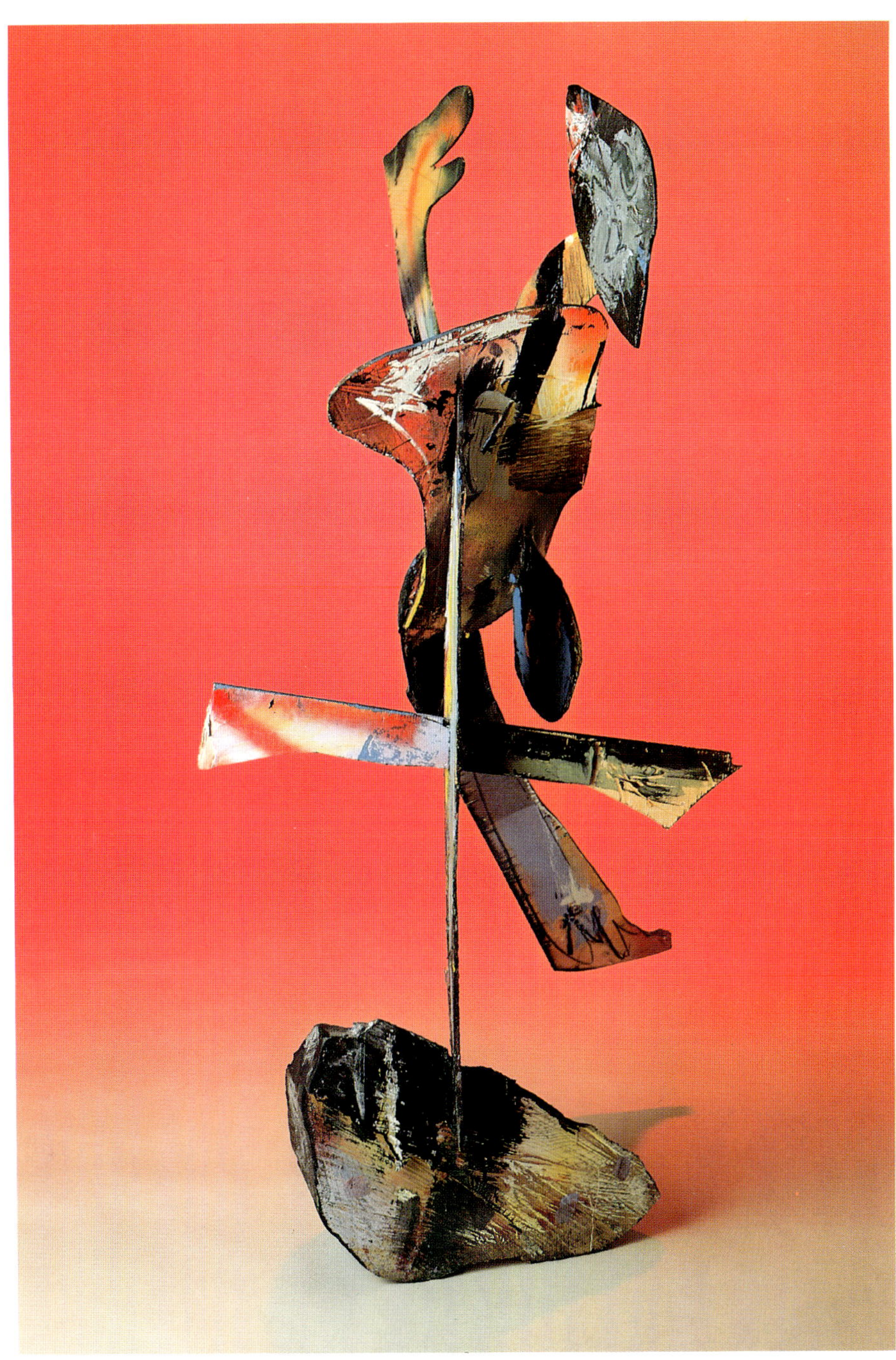

Balancing Act   Mary Beth Fogarty, 48 x 36 x 2.5 in., painted wood.

I paint realism as I feel it.

With minimal planning,
I get into a painting immediately establishing the composition,
color relationships and values.
Excitement grows in the refinement process, working from
dark to light, positive to negative and from chaos to simplicity.
Bringing a painting to its conclusion gives me a sense of
peace and fulfillment.

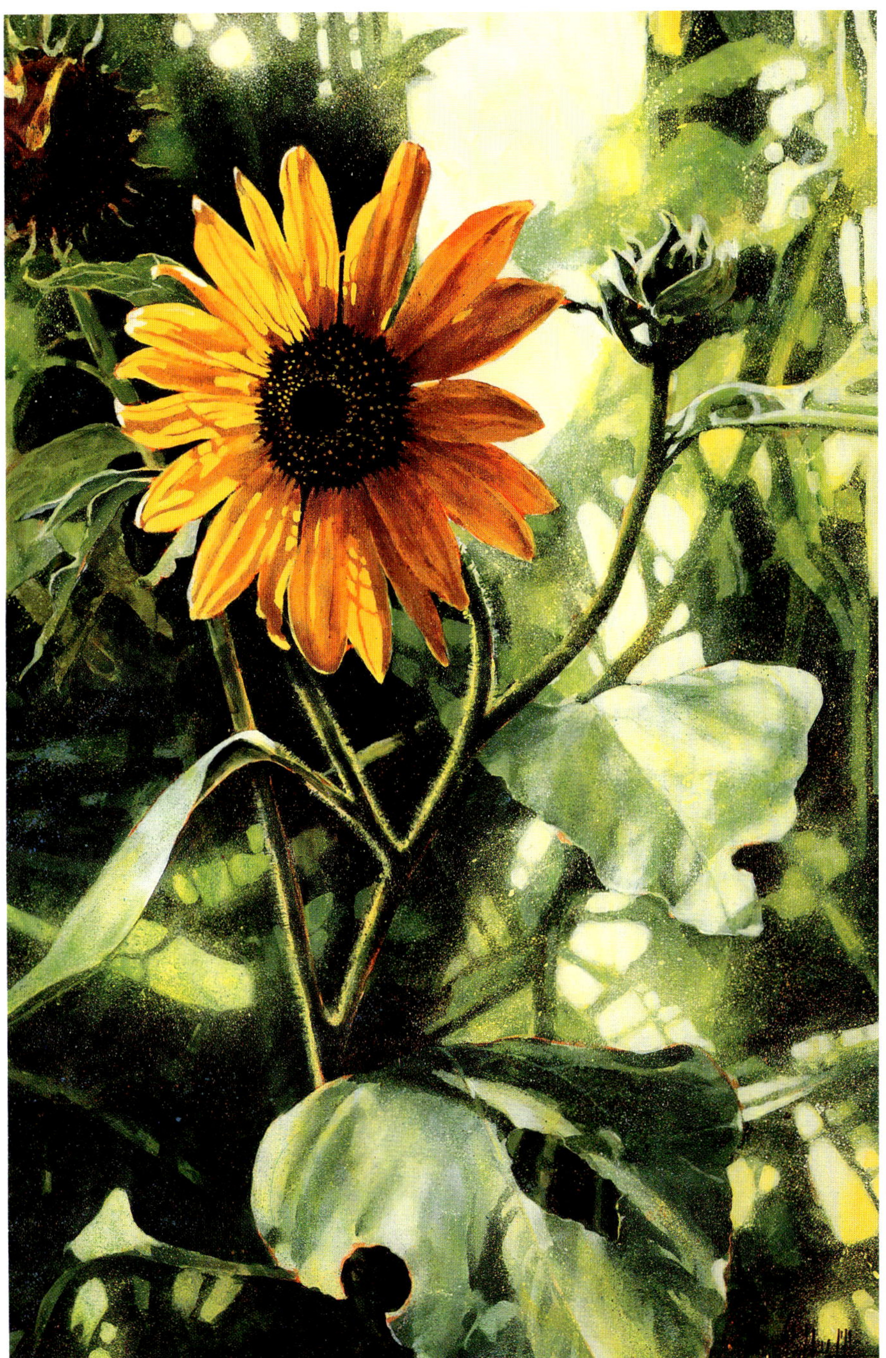

Sundance Judy Greff, 48 x 32 in., acrylic.

*I am interested in color
and patterns of light. Using
these elements, I attempt to
distill my way of experiencing
the landscape onto the flat
surface of paper or canvas.
If I can succeed in this effort,
perhaps the viewer will come
away from my work with a
new way of seeing the world
around him.*

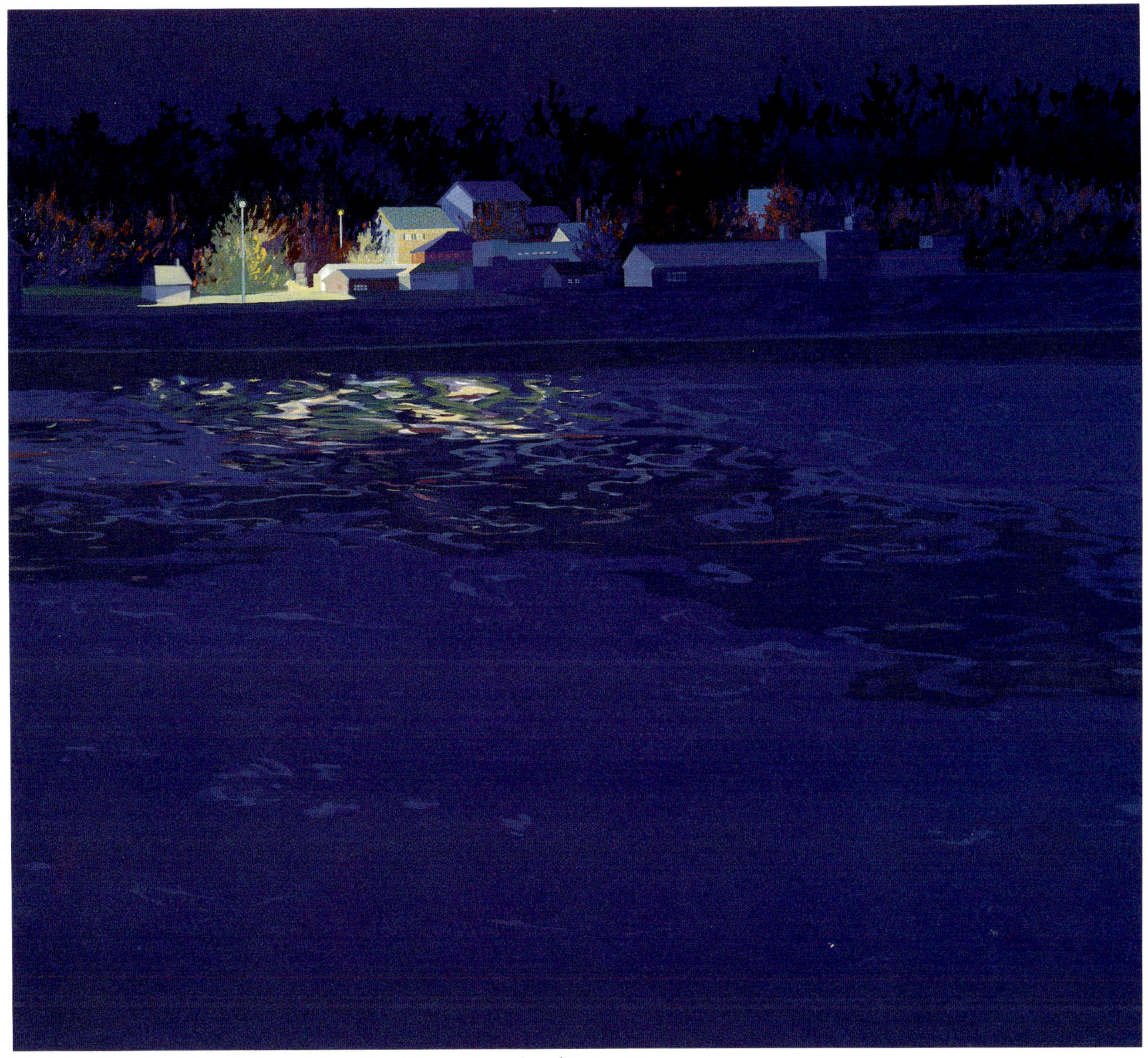

The Other Side of the Lake   Barbara Kastner, 39 x 45 in., casein and acrylic on paper.

I don't attempt to portray the land in a realistic manner, although a bird's eye view looking into the Missouri River valley is amazingly like my compositions - very "hard-edge" in appearance, rich in design, with subtle variations and bold contrasts and resplendent with a wide variety of color and value.

As I construct a painting, I'm more interested in capturing an intriguing composition, in using the interaction of trees, land, plowed fields and terraces and I search for a kind of solitude - an openness. My work of the last few years has a dramatic quality, but also a serene appeal.

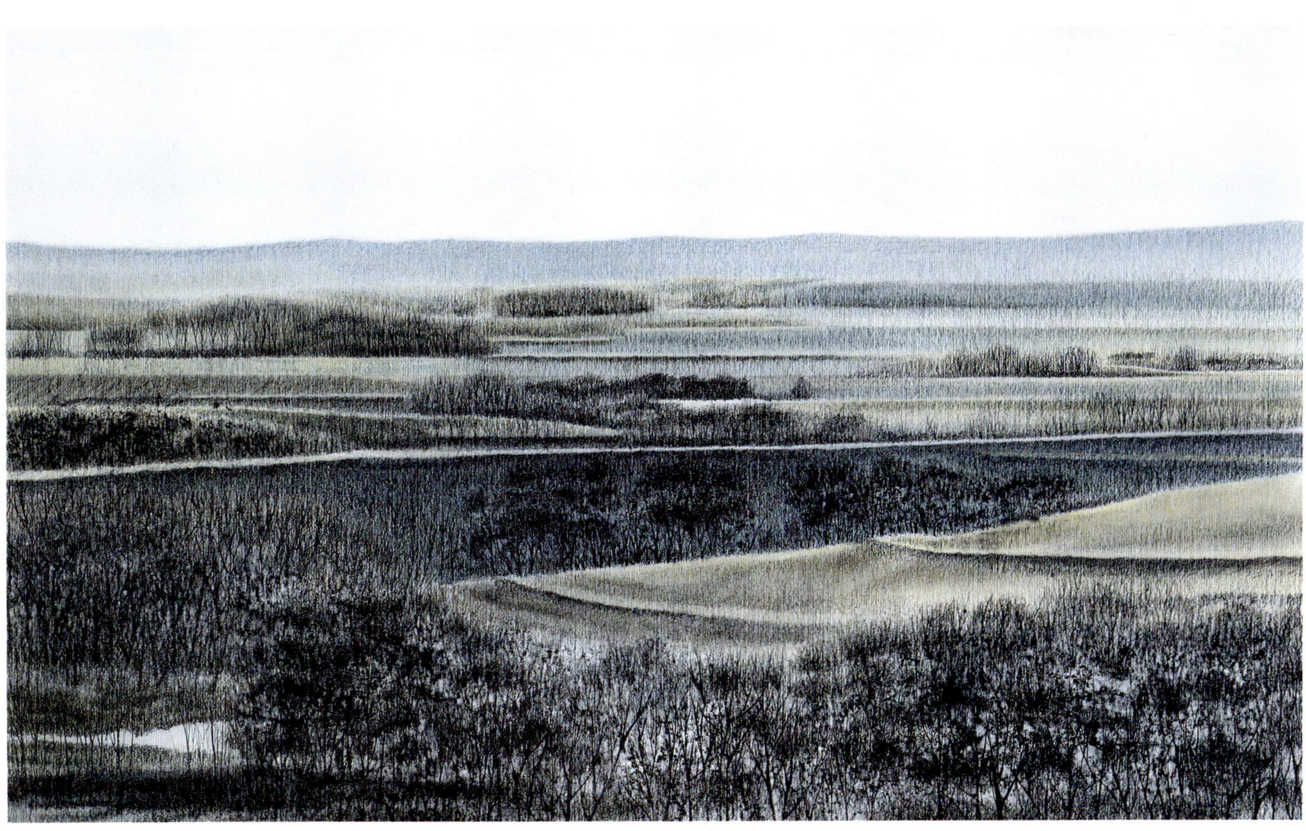

Between the Lines   Deborah J. Murphy, 18 x 31 in., graphite, solvent and prismacolor.

Inspiration for my paintings comes naturally and involves design and familiarity of subject matter, be it vegetation, flowers and garden, collectables, family members or area scenes. Travel is an intricate part of my life, therefore, other areas of the world are also captured in my art.

Painting creatively for me is a continual learning experience: making visual statements, capturing an emotional impact or a memorable event in time, striving always for excellence in this chosen life-style of producing art.

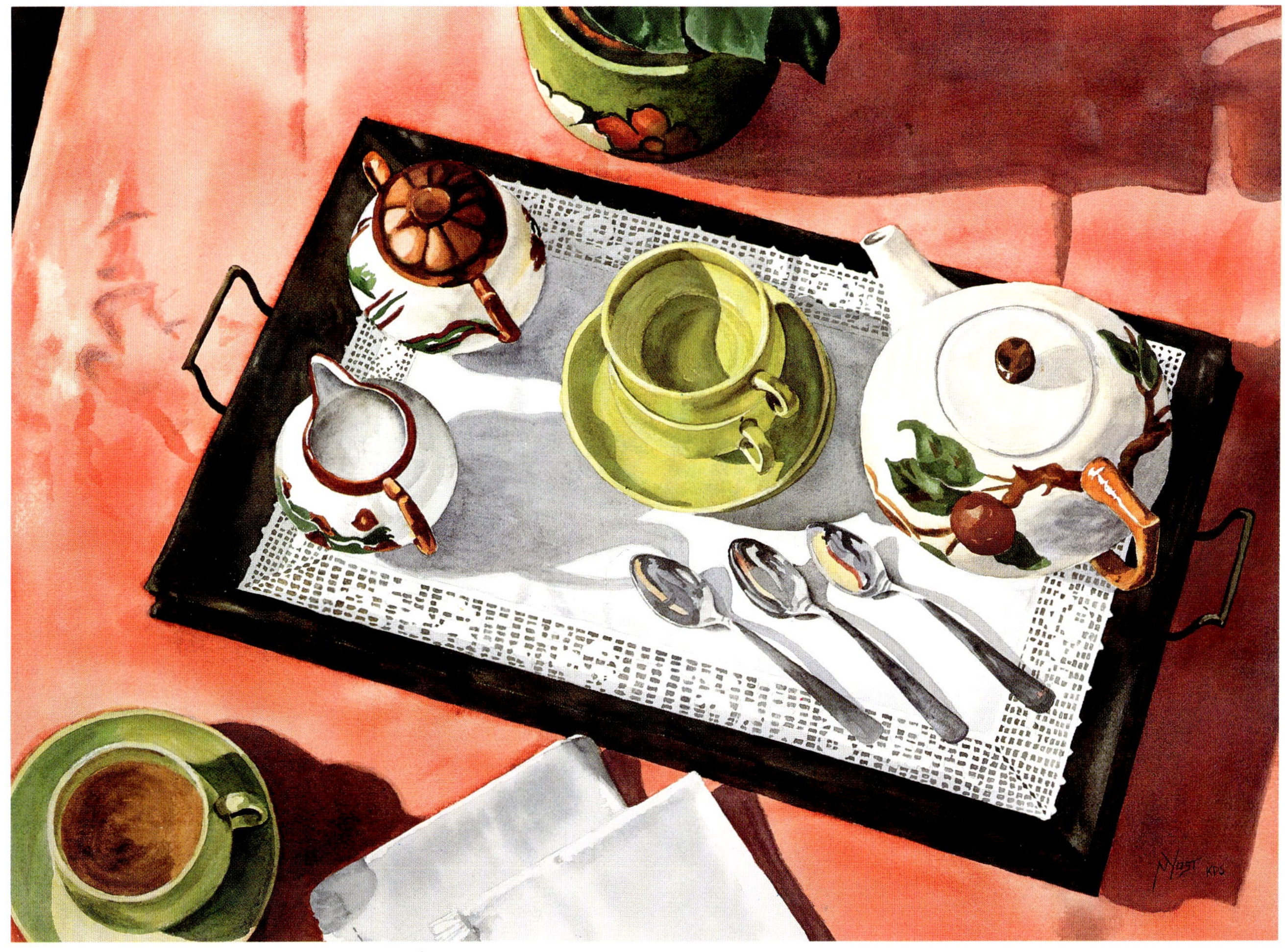

Three for Tea   Maxine Yost, 21 x 29 in., watercolor.

My mixed media constructions evolve from an accumulation of objects in my life. They are selected and collected because of personal interest. I am interested in the physical characteristics of the objects, their shape and texture.

The assembled constructions have the feeling of being cultural artifacts.

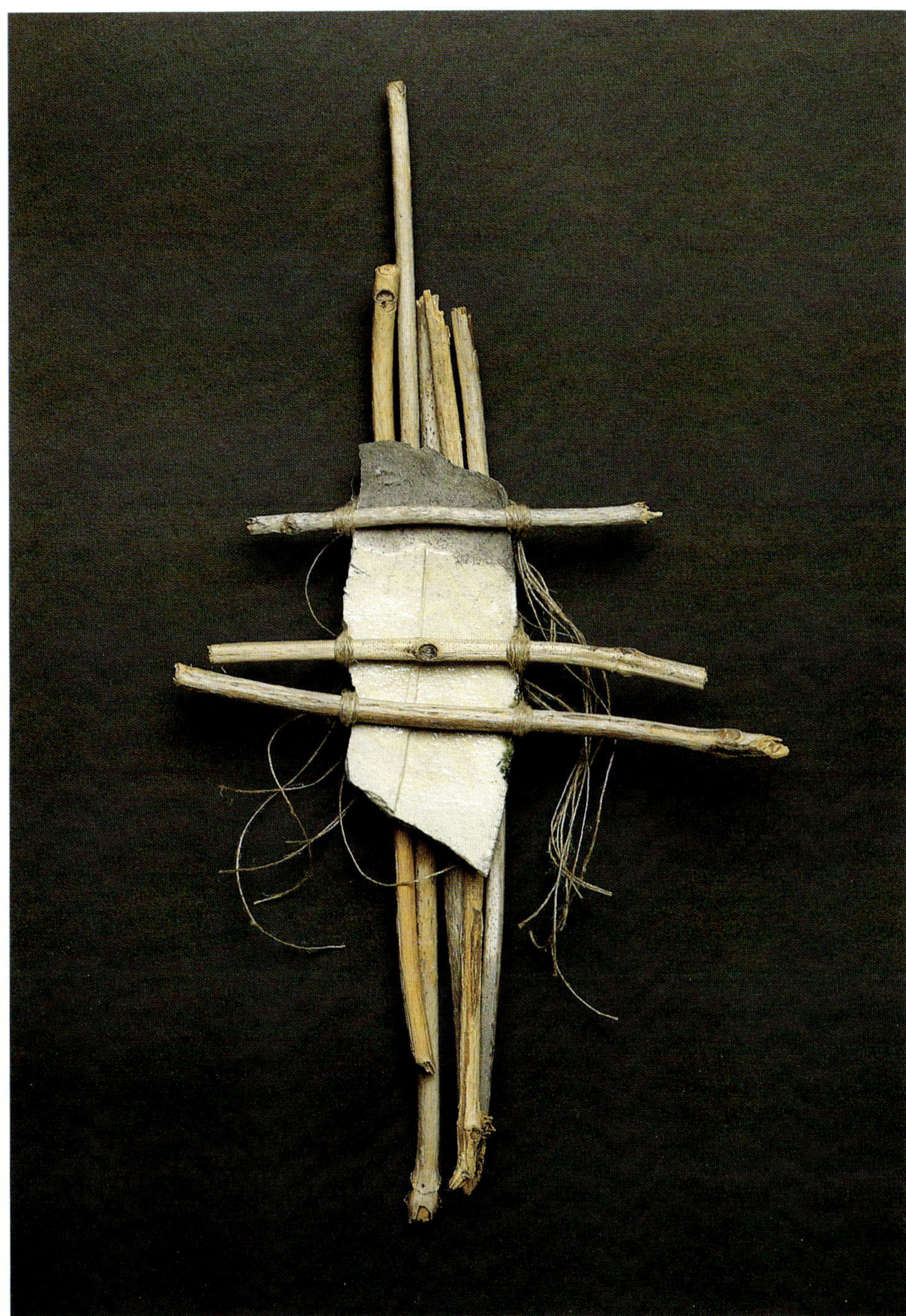

Fragment I   Margie A. Schimenti, 14 x 7 in., wood, clay, cord.

Index of Artists

Baltzer-Jacobo, Bobbie - 1946 Page 34.
4523 Charles Street   Omaha, NE   68132
*Commissioned to Paint Original Boystown
Home,* from Boystown Middle School,
Boystown, Nebr.
*Conversations with Nebraska Women Artists:
Book,* interviewed by Lu O'Connell.
*Purchase Award in "American Art; the
Challenge of the Land" Pillsbury Corp.,* St. Paul,
Minn.
Merit Award — Midwest Biennial, Joslyn Art
Museum, Omaha, Nebr.
Recent Realism — Show, Buffalo, N.Y.

Benton, Linda K. - 1946 Page 60.
Earth Song Farm Rt. 1 Box 54
Greenwood, NE   68366
*Drawing published ARABIAN HORSE WORLD
magazine*
Langworthy Watercolor Show Seward,
Ne. Award and purchase
"OUR LIVES: THE EXPERIENCE OF WOMEN"
Un. of Kansas Lawrence, Ks.
R.G. Dickerson "PORTFOLIO SHOW"
Omaha, Ne.
Represented Nebraska Art Collection
Kearney, Ne.

Bower, Marilyn - 1941 Page 58.
922 North Second Street   Seward, NE   68434
Joslyn Art Museum, 19th Biennial Exhibition, NE
Spiva Art Center, 35th Competition Exhibition,
MO
Fred Wells Annual Exhibition, 8 and 10th, NE
Nebraska "Reflections" Exhibitions, 3, 4, & 6th,
Purchase Award
*Langworthy Art Competition, 4 years, Best of
Show,* Purchase Award, NE

Burkholder, Anne - 1940 Page 18.
719 P St.   Lincoln, NE   68508
Watercolor USA, Springfield, Missouri,
2 Purchase Awards
Solo Shows: Minneapolis Art Institute, Friends
Gallery, Minnesota 1984, 1982
*"American Art: The Challenge of the Land,"
Pillsbury Company,* Minneapolis, Minnesota,
Purchase Award
"Mid-Four Annual Juried Art Exhibition,"
Nelson-Atkins Museum, Kansas City, Missouri,
1983
13th, 18th Joslyn Biennial, Omaha, Nebraska

Chapin, Nancy Childs - 1951 Page 30.
719 P Street   Lincoln, NE   68508
Professional Women Artist's Invitational,
Nebraska, 2 years
Printmaker's Show III, Washington, D.C.
The Eye of Hartigan, Washington, D.C.
Octagon Clay and Paper Exhibit, Iowa
Kansas One Exhibition, Kansas

Day, Mary; M.F.A. - 1948 Page 6.
5621 Erskine St.   Omaha, NE 68104
Printmakers Invitational, Cameron University,
Lawton, Oklahoma
*Small Sculpture Invitational: Works by
Women,* University of Cincinnatti, Ohio
Rutgers National on Paper, Rutgers University,
Camden, New Jersey
Appalachian National, Appalachian State
University, Boone, North Carolina
Women Artists Today, University of South
Dakota at Vermillion, Purchase Prize

Devlin, Susan; B.F.A. - 1947 Page 48.
3710 South 117th St.   Omaha, NE   68144
Fall Biennial Sioux City Art Center, Sioux City,
Iowa
Invitational Women's Art Exhibit, Indiana
University, Bloomington, Indiana
National Juried Competition, Montana
Institute of the Arts, Billings, Montana
Regional Juried Art Exhibition, University of
South Dakota, Vermillion, South Dakota
Invitational Art Exhibit, Cathedral Art Gallery,
Omaha, Nebraska

Dienstbier, Karen; M.F.A. - 1941 Page 22.
501 Dale Dr.   Lincoln, NE   68510
1987 Biennial Sioux City Art Center, Sioux
City, Iowa
Mid-Four Exhibit. Nelson-Atkins Museum of
Art, K.C., MO. Merit Award. 1984
7th Annual "Bridges" Exhibition. Grumbacher
Award, Best of Show. NE. 1982
American Art — The Challenge of the Land:
Purchase Award, Minn., MN. 1981
MFA Thesis Exhibition. Sheldon Memorial Art
Gallery. Lincoln, NE. 1979

Farrar, Michele Angle - 1943 Page 44.
1917 Pawnee,   Lincoln, NE   68502
U.S. Department of Education, Washington, D.C., commissioned work, 1980
Association of Conservation Information, 1st place design award for Nebraska Through the Seasons, 1980.
Association of Conservation Information, 1st place design award for NEBRASKAland Magazine, 1981.
Nebraska Wesleyan University, Fred Wells Juried Show, purchase award, 1980 Judge's Award, 1981, 1987.
Indoor Plants published by John Wiley & Sons, N.Y. 1987, Botanical illustrations.

Fogarty, Mary Beth; A.A., B.A., M.F.A. -1943 Page 64.
503 No. 38th St.   Omaha, NE   68132
Art and Artist in Nebraska, Norman Geske, published in association with the Center For Great Plains Studies
Contemporary American Women Sculptors: Bio-Bibliographical Directory
"The Governor's Arts Awards - An Exhibition," Lincoln, Nebraska
Nominated for an AWA Award in the Visual Arts, national artists award
Sheldon Memorial Art Gallery, Lincoln, Nebraska, solo exhibition

Golden, Dona Lee; B.F.A., M.A. - 1931 Page 36.
2142 South 108th St.   Omaha, NE   68144
Print Show, Award, Signal Hills, St. Paul, Mn.
Nebraska Invitational, Joslyn Museum, Omaha, Ne.
14th Biennial, Joslyn Museum, Omaha, Ne.
Nebraska Art Educators Art Show, Elder Gallery, Lincoln, Ne.
Association of Nebraska Art Clubs, Purchase Award, Lincoln, Ne.

Greff, Judy - 1941 Page 66.
407 South Sixth Avenue   Burwell, NE   68823
Allied Artists of America Gold Medal of Honor, 74th Annual Exhibition, New York, New York
Elected Member, National Society of Painters in Casein and Acrylic; New York, New York
Elected Member, Catharine Lorillard Wolfe Art Club; New York, New York
Nebraska Art Collection, Museum of Nebraska Art; Kearney,Nebraska
Permanent Collection, Nebraska Wesleyan University; Lincoln, Nebraka
Nebraska Art Collection, Museum of Nebraska Art; Kearney, Nebraska

Hagge, Dora; K.A. - 1942 Page 32.
1224 Sheridan Drive   Hastings, NE   68901
Elected Member of Knickerbocker Artists, New York, New York
National Watercolor Society 66th Annual, Award, Traveling Exhibition, California
Knickerbocker Artists 37th Exhibition, Salmagundi Club, New York City
Catherine Lorillard Wolfe 90th Exhibition, Award, New York City
Southwestern Watercolor Society 22nd, 26th Exhibitions, Texas

Hajny, Desiree; B.A., N.W.C.A., A.W.L. 1957 Page 56.
3212 Mueller Dr.   Columbus, NE   68601
Elected Member of The Guild of Master Craftsmen International, East Sussex, England
Canadian International Wood Carving, 10th, 11th Exhibitions, Awards; Toronto, Ontario
International Woodcarvers Congress, Awards; Bettendorf, IA
Great Plains Carving Exhibition, Judges Choice, Awards, Wichita, KS.
The Alaskan Shop, Vail, Co.; Branson Clockworks Gallery, Mountain Woodcarvers Gallery, Branson, MO.

Kastner, Barbara - 1936 Page 68.
3629 South 77th Street   Lincoln, NE   68506
National Academy of Design 159th Annual Exhibition, NY;
American Watercolor Society (elected member) 118th, 116th & traveling exhibition 115th, 110th, NY
Allied Artists of America 73rd, 74th Exhibitions, Award, NY
National Watercolor Society (elected member) 61st, 62nd Exhibitions, Award, traveling exhibitions
Watercolor USA, Rocky Mountain National Watermedia Exhibitions, numerous other national, regional and invitational exhibitions Watercolor

Kunc, Karen; B.F.A., M.F.A. - 1952 Page 52.
RR #1, Box #71   Avoca, NE   68307
Mid-America Arts Alliance/National Endowment for the Arts Visual Arts Fellowship
Solo Exhibition, Sheldon Memorial Art Gallery, Lincoln, Nebraska
Visiting Professor, University of California, Berkeley
Guest Artist, US Information Agency, conducting workshops & lectures in Finland and Poland
First Prize Award, Graphica Atlantica, Reykjavik, Iceland

Lynn, Sammy J. - 1937 Page 46.
R.R. 1 Box 178   Glenvil, NE   68941
"Prairie Treasures" Joslyn Art Museum,
Omaha, NE
The Wichita National '86, '87 Wichita, KA
Eureka Springs Art and Craft Fair Annual,
10th, 11th, Eureka Springs, AR, First Place,
3 Dimension
Association of Nebraska Art Clubs, Purchase
Award, Nebr. Permanent Collection

MacKichan, Margaret A.; B.F.A., M.F.A. -
1948 Page 24.
2570 Woods Blvd.   Lincoln, NE   68502
Mid-America Arts Alliance/National
Endowment for the Arts Fellowship
Nebraska Arts Council and Nebraska
Committee on the Humanities Grant
International Museum of Photography at the
George Eastman House Internship
Society of Contemporary Photography Award
Royal Academy Exhibition, Edinburgh,
Scotland

Murphy, Deborah J.; B.A. - 1950 Page 70.
3119 North 58th Street   Omaha, NE   68104
Biennial, Sioux City Art Center, Sioux City, Iowa
Galex 21, Galesburg Civic Art Center, Illinois,
Award
American Art Annual, Middletown Fine Arts
Center, Ohio, two years
Second Women in Art Competition, Springfield
Art Gallery, Illinois
Art Annual Three, Oklahoma Art Center,
Oklahoma City, Oklahoma

Murphy, Mary Catania; B.S. - 1949
Page 26.
6720 Davenport St.   Omaha, NE   68132
20th Joslyn Biennial, 1988 Exhibition, Omaha
R.G. Dickinson & Co. 1986 Portfolio's
Exhibition, Omaha
One Woman Show, Bemis Project/Alternative
Worksite, 1986, Omaha
St. Cecilia's Cathedral Centennial Invitational
Art Exhibition 1988, Omaha
1985 "Reflections" ANAC Competition,
Kearney, NE

Olson-Mandler, Sue; N.W.S. - 1941
Page 38.
515 Ridgewood Dr.   Bellevue, NE   68005
National Watercolor Society 63rd Annual, 1983;
San Diego Watercolor Society Int. Exhibit 1983
Butler Institute of American Art, 48th,
49th Annual National Midyear Shows,
Youngstown, OH

Artist for Omaha's Sister City Assoc. in Shizouka,
Japan, 1985
"Bob Hope and Friends" record album cover,
1981; Christmas at Boys Town, 1978
Published in "WEST/Art and the Law", West
Publishing Co. law related corporate art
collection, St. Paul, MN

Pettit, Carol - 1932 Page 42.
Rt #1   Greenwood, NE   68366
Featured article - American Artist Magazine
Nebraska 75 - Joslyn Art Museum, Omaha, NE
NE Humane Society Centennial - Omaha, NE
Award
6 State Art Exhibition - College of St. Mary,
Omaha, NE, Award
Sioux City Biennial - Sioux City, IA

Puelz, Susan P.; B.F.A., M.F.A. - 1942
Page 12.
3120 Prescott Ave.   Lincoln, NE   68502
Recipient of Midwest Arts Alliance and
National Endowment for the Arts Fellowship
Award in Painting;
Watercolor U.S.A. National Traveling
Exhibition;
Charter Member of Watercolor U.S.A. Honor
Society (membership limited to Award
Winners and jurors of Watercolor U.S.A.;
First place, watercolor, Art Quest '85 University
Art Museum of California State University,
Long Beach, CA.;
Vreeland Award, University of Nebraska

Sadle, Amy A. - 1940 Page 50.
2918 14th Street   Columbus, NE   68601
Woodcut in the Permanent Collection of the
Statue of Liberty
San Diego Print Club, Invitational Show and
Top Award in Competition
Who's Who of American Women and
Outstanding Young Women of America
Feature Story, in Grumbacher's "Palette Talk"
Daniel Smith Grant for the Research in
Metallic Products in Art

Schimenti, Margie A.; B.A., M.A. - 1949
Page 74.
   1006 Howard St., Apt. 2 Omaha, NE 68102
Biennial Exhibition, Sioux City Art Center,
Sioux City, Iowa
Fifth Holiday Invitational Exhibit, A.I.R.
Gallery, New York City
*Regional Artists Invitational, 1st and 2nd
Exhibitions,* Cathedral Gallery, Omaha,
Nebraska
*Nebraska Crafts Council Exhibition at the
Nebraska Museum of Art,* Award, Kearney,
Nebraska
Biennial Sioux City Art Center, All Media
Competitive, Sioux City, Iowa

Scott, Jane; P.S.A. Page 8.
   1402 South Skyline Dr. Elkhorn, NE 68022
Member of Pastel Society of America, Awards
in 4 National Exhibits, 3rd, 8th, 11th, 15th
*Elected Master Pastelist in Pastel Society of
America,* Exhibits in USA, France
Member of Catharine Lorillard Wolfe Art Club,
Three National Awards, NY, 81, 84, 89
*Allied Artists of America, 67th, 70th, National
Exhibits,* New York, NY
*Published in Artists Of The Rockies, and
American Artist*

Shindell, Mary; B.F.A., M.F.A. - 1949
Page 28.
   307 S. 51st Street Omaha, NE 68132
Women in Art, A National Invitational, Illinois
Invitational Show of Contemporary Artists,
Maryland
Spokane National, Works on Paper,
Washington
Twenty Arizona Artists, Phoenix Art Museum,
Arizona
6th National Print and Drawing Exhibition,
North Dakota

Smith, Patsy - 1939 Page 10.
   821 Apache Drive North Platte, NE 69101
*Orange County Watercolor Society National
Exhibition, 11th Annual,* New York
*North American Artist Association Annual
Juried Show,* 1st Place, Colorado
National American Mothers Art Exhibit, 2nd
Place, Louisiana
Kansas Watercolor Society Exhibition, Kansas
American Painters in Paris Exhibition, France

Snyder, Charlotte S. - 1922 Page 14.
   R.R. 2, Box 176, Minatare, NE 69356
*International Miniature Art Exh., 6th & 9th
Annual,* Awards, Florida
*International Miniature Art Exh., 7th, 10th,
13th Annual,* Awards, New Jersey
National NPVAG Art Exhibition, Best of Show
Award, Nebraska
North American Mycological Assn. Exh.,
Dartmouth College, New Hampshire
Elected signature member, Whiskey Painters of
America, Ohio

Soloway, Lynn - 1946 Page 54.
   4900 West Benton Lincoln, NE 68524
*Terrance Gallery Annual National Drawing
Exhibition,* Award, Palenville, NY
*American Slide Library of Contemporary Arts
and Crafts Exhibition,* Palm Beach, FL
Watercolor USA, Springfield Art Museum,
Springfield, MO
*33rd, 45th National Annual Exhibitions,
Butler Institute of American Art,* Youngstown,
OH
Black Hills Multi State Exhibition, Best of
Show, First Place Graphics, Rapid City, SD

Stonecipher, LaDell Routh; B.A., B.F.A. -
1940
Page 16.
   711 West 1st Hastings, NE 68901
Invitational Shows, Batman Gallery, Kansas
City, Mo.
Collections: V. Nikonev, Sec. of Agric., Soviet
Union
West Publishing Co., St. Paul, Minnesota
NE Arts Council Artist-in-Schools: Omaha,
No. Platte, Gr. Island, Friend
Nebr. Women's Art Exhibit, Awards, Omaha &
No. Platte

Wattles, Virginia; K.P.S., B.A., M.A. - 1939
Page 62.
   Grumbacher Silver Medal, Kansas Pastel
Society 4th Intenational Pastel Exhibition
Best of Show; Nebraska Art Educator Exhibit
Elected Signature Member, Kansas Pastel
Society
Exhibitor, First, Third, Fourth Kansas Pastel
Society National Exhibition
Exhibitor, Fred Wells Ten State Juried
Exhibition

Welstead, Jean M.; N.L.A.P.W. - 1922 Page 20.
1943 Parkview Drive   Fremont, NE   68025
Nebraska Permanent Art Collection, Kearney, Nebraska, Purchase Award.
Wayne State College National Competitive, Permanent Collection, Award, Wayne, NE
National League of American Pen Woman, Inc. National Biennial, Award, Washington, D.C.
Nebraska Wesleyan University Regional Competitive, Permanent Collection, Purchase Award
Appalachian National Drawing Competition, Purchase Award, Boone, North Carolina

Yost, Maxine; K.P.S. - 1918 Page 72.
915 West B   North Platte, NE   69101
Catharine Lorillard Wolfe 90th Exhibition, New York
Served as President (2 years), Association of Nebraska Art Clubs, Inc.
Kansas Pastel Society, signature member
Nebraska Art Collection, Museum of Nebraska Art
Midwest Watercolor Society, 10th Annual, Wisconsin

Youngquist, Lynelle - 1959 Page 40.
Box 428   Orleans, NE   68966
Fine Art For Fine Causes, Exhibition & Auction, Tucson, AZ
Dane G. Hansen Memorial Museum, Two Person Show, Logan, KS
Michigan ARTRAIN, Demonstrating & Exhibiting Artist, Lincoln, NE
The Lincoln Symphony/A.S.I.D. Showhouse Benefit, Lincoln, NE
Haymarket Art Gallery, Three Person Show, Lincoln, NE

Acknowledgements

Patrons

Woods Charitable Fund, Inc.	Behlen Manufacturing
Rapid Printing & Mailing, Inc.	George Neubert

Underwrite

Marvin and Jean Welstead	Larry & Patsy Smith
Gwendolyn McKenzie	Jack and Amy Sadle

Benefactors

ConAgra Charitable Foundation, Inc.	Columbus Library
Duncan Aviation, Inc.	Thomas Creigh, Jr.
Douglas and Lomason Co., Columbus Branch	Tran-Tec Corporation

Friends

Northwestern Bell Foundation	Terrance McGrane
American Society of Interior Designers, NE/IA Chapter	Greg Bauer
First National Bank & Trust Company, Columbus	Tamara Buntgen
First Federal Lincoln, Lincoln	Dr. Gary Zaruba
National League of American Pen Women, Omaha Branch	Marcella Dvorak
Columbus Area Artists	Steve Settles Foundry
Burwell Brush Busters	Amy Sadle Studio
Bellevue Artists's Association, Inc.	Sue Olson-Mandler
Box Butte Art Society	Dora Hagge
Mr. & Mrs. W.W. Cook	Judy Greff
Mr. & Mrs. Bernie Taylor	Catherine L. Sansoni
Mrs. Norris V. Swan	Karen Dienstbier
Gretchen Garwood	Marilyn Bower
Clifford B. Cox	Charlotte Snyder
Lesley Loutzenheiser	Jean Welstead
Mary Collins	Desiree Hajny
Cheyenne County Art Guild	Patsy Smith
Gretchen Hollman Lainson	Gary L. Gruenemeier
Anne Wagner	

IMPACT, Inc. acknowledges those listed above, who through their commitment to the arts in Nebraska and their support have made this publication possible.

We would like to express our thanks and appreciation to our husbands, Hank Greff, Jerry Hagge, Stan Mandler and Jack Sadle for their patience and positive support they provided throughout this project.

The Editors